New International
A MAGAZINE OF MARXIST POLITICS AND THEORY

NUMBER 2   WINTER 1983–84

Contents

In this issue   *3*

The working-class fight for peace
by Brian Grogan   *13*

The development of the Marxist position on the aristocracy of labor
by Steve Clark   *99*

ARSENAL OF MARXISM

The social roots of opportunism
by Gregory Zinoviev   *165*

Index   *247*

EDITORIAL BOARD Steve Clark, Malik Miah, Joan Newbigging, Steve Penner, José G. Perez, John Riddell, Larry Seigle, John Steele, Mary-Alice Waters

Copyright © 1983 by New International

All rights reserved
ISSN 0737-3724
ISBN 978-0-87348-637-8
Manufactured in Canada

First printing, 1983
Sixth printing, 2022

IN THIS ISSUE

THIS SECOND ISSUE of *New International* focuses on several political themes that were central to discussions at the Socialist Educational and Activists Conference held in Oberlin, Ohio, in August 1983. That conference was attended by more than 1,000 socialists from the United States and Canada, as well as from some twenty other countries.

Pointing to the revolutionary victory in Cuba a quarter century ago, and the coming to power of workers and farmers governments in Nicaragua and Grenada in 1979, U.S. Socialist Workers Party National Secretary Jack Barnes explained in the opening talk at the conference that "the reality of the living, ongoing American socialist revolution, fighting arms in hand to extend itself and defend itself," is at the heart of the political prospects and challenges of socialist workers in North America.

The showdown between U.S. imperialism and the workers and peasants of Central America and the Caribbean is the starting point for the first article in this issue, "The Working-Class Fight for Peace." It is an edited version of a talk by Brian Grogan at the August conference.

Grogan is a British member of the United Secretariat of the Fourth International.

The U.S. invasion of Grenada, the sharp escalation of the counterrevolutionary war against Nicaragua, and the direct use of U.S. and other imperialist military power in Lebanon during the months since the August conference all drive home the importance of the political themes developed by Grogan. The source of wars and the threat of war is the drive by the U.S. and other imperialist ruling classes to defeat and roll back the gains of national liberation struggles and victorious workers and farmers governments, Grogan explains. That is why the class battles today over the extension of the socialist revolution in Central America and the Caribbean are at the very center of world politics.

As Grogan points out, it is also imperialism's determination to crush the revolutionary struggles by workers and peasants in the Americas, in the Middle East, in Indochina, and around the world that threatens at some point to lead to a nuclear war resulting in mass annihilation.

Working people cannot lessen the chance of a nuclear war by shrinking in fear before the awesome power of the imperialists, Grogan explains. To the contrary, that only emboldens the exploiters. The only road to world peace is to beat back the imperialists and deal them defeats, as the people of Vietnam did in the 1960s and 1970s. These are the stakes in Central America and the Caribbean today, as well. Each victory for the world revolution weakens the capitalist warmakers and pushes back the prospects for new wars by them that could lead to a nuclear holocaust.

Ultimately, as Grogan explains, the only guarantee against such a catastrophe for humanity is for the U.S.

working class to lead its oppressed and exploited allies in a revolution that can wrest political power—including the power to make war—from the hands of the capitalist rulers and establish a workers and farmers government. Only then will the American socialist revolution initiated twenty-five years ago in Cuba be completed and secure.

THIS RELATES to another major theme of the August conference—the gap between the advance of the socialist revolution in Central America and the Caribbean and the continuing lag in the level of class struggle and political consciousness in the imperialist countries, including the United States.

The other two items in this issue of *New International* are aimed at equipping revolutionary workers with some important political and theoretical tools that can help them understand this gap and participate as effective working-class fighters and politicians in the struggles that can begin to close it.

In our "Arsenal of Marxism" department this issue, we are republishing a translation of major excerpts from a 1916 article by Russian Bolshevik leader Gregory Zinoviev on the role of the labor aristocracy and labor bureaucracy in the degeneration of the German Social Democratic Party during the period leading up to World War I. The first English translation of the article appeared in the May–June 1942 issues of the *New International*, a journal then published by the Workers Party, led by Max Shachtman. This translation has been revised by *NI* editor John Riddell. Zinoviev's article was originally published in *Voina i krizis sotsializma (The War and the Crisis of Social Democracy)*.

The other item, written as a companion to the Zinoviev article by *NI* editor Steve Clark, traces the development of the Marxist understanding of the labor aristocracy and discusses a number of questions posed by it for the program and strategy of the revolutionary workers movement.

The usefulness of the matters discussed in these two articles was highlighted during the August conference in talks by Jack Barnes and by SWP National Chairperson Barry Sheppard, as well as by the discussions at the meeting of the Socialist Workers Party's National Committee directly following the conference.

"We are in a preparatory period prior to the working class challenging the imperialists for power," Barnes explained in the opening talk to the conference. It is a period, he said, during which the cadres are being assembled to construct a revolutionary working-class party capable of leading that struggle for power against the strongest and most ruthless ruling class in world history. In this period, these initial cadres will gain valuable experience and learn how to apply the Marxist program and strategy as participants and revolutionary propagandists in the class struggle.

The only way to gather those cadres and prepare them for the tasks that lie ahead, Barnes said, is to build "a party deeply committed to and deeply part of the struggles of the working class and rooted in its strongest organizations as they exist today."

THE CURRENT SITUATION in U.S. politics and the labor movement was the topic of Sheppard's talk. He pointed out that the U.S. working class entered into a long political retreat during the first two and a half decades following World War II. During that period, the officialdom of the mass industrial unions, forged through big class battles in the 1930s, entrenched its position as a consolidated bureaucratic layer. This process had already gone a long way through the bureaucrats' cooperation with the bosses and the imperialist government during the war.

As the U.S. capitalists launched the "cold war" to contain and roll back national liberation struggles and the extension of the socialist revolution abroad, they initiated a broadside attack against democratic rights at home. At the center of this witch-hunt was a purge of militants and socialists from the unions—conducted with the collaboration of the big majority of U.S. union officials.

The housebreaking of U.S. labor was not and could not have been achieved through repression and victimization alone, however. The political retreat of U.S. labor in the 1950s and 1960s was grounded in the prolonged period of economic expansion made possible by the predominant position of U.S. imperialism as a military, industrial, and trading power coming out of World War II. The resulting margin for concessions by the employing class to substantial layers of the working class facilitated the institutionalization of class-collaborationist methods on a broad scale in the labor movement.

Labor's efforts centered on maintaining and slowly but steadily improving the living standards of those sections of the working class that had already been unionized; no sustained efforts were made to organize the unorganized, and the percentage of unionized workers declined from year to year. Instead of fighting for adequate nationwide government-funded health, retirement, and unemployment benefits to protect the working population as a whole, unions were increasingly drawn into industry-by-industry agreements that tied workers' benefits to the bosses' profits.

Job trusts that barred oppressed nationalities and women from certain trades, unions, and job categories in industry became further consolidated. Meanwhile, the unions did little relative to their potential power to help, let alone lead, the growing fight for Black civil rights during those years. The AFL-CIO officialdom became a mainstay for the bipartisan foreign policy of the U.S. ruling class, even collaborating intimately with the CIA against the labor movement in many countries.

Tying together this expanding web of class collaboration, the labor officialdom kept the unions and the working class hitched to the capitalist two-party system. There was no motion toward, and practically no discussion of, an independent labor party based on the unions.

The class struggle began to be revitalized in the United States in the late 1950s and 1960s, but the progress did not originate inside the organized labor movement. It began with the mass struggles for Black rights, and later the movement against the war in Vietnam. These struggles, and the new rise in the fight for women's emancipation, affected millions of workers and began to be reflected inside the labor movement in the 1970s.

MOREOVER, the prolonged U.S. capitalist expansion came to a definitive end with the worldwide depression of 1974–75. The years since then, despite periodic upturns in the business cycle, have been marked by cutbacks in social services, attacks on gains won by Blacks and women, rising unemployment levels, and take-back contracts in basic industry. It remains a period in which the employers are imposing defensive battles on working people, and in which setbacks and defeats for the unions are still much more frequent than victories.

These factors have all combined to deepen the class polarization in U.S. politics and have led to the *beginnings* of a radicalization of the U.S. working class and of changes in the unions. This radicalization, however, is still limited and uneven.

Barnes pointed out that the writings by Marx, Engels, and Lenin on the labor aristocracy provide part of the political equipment revolutionists need today to understand both the political retreat of the U.S. working class during the quarter century following World War II and the forms taken by the developing process of radicalization and polarization affecting the U.S. working class and its various strata. Throughout the period since World War II, as during the years leading up to World War I, Barnes said, "a layer of the working class in the imperialist countries that had the most steady employment and received the best wages" became convinced "that to one degree or another their future and the future of their families lay with tying themselves to their bosses, not to other workers—especially the colonial peoples."

These relatively better-off workers in the United States represented quite a sizeable layer in the postwar period. The labor bureaucracy based itself largely on these sections of the working class and found in them the best audience for its class-collaborationist perspectives. While the political and economic shocks of the last decade have narrowed this layer and begun to shake up the U.S. labor movement, that process is still in its early stages.

This understanding of the relationship of the labor aristocracy and labor bureaucracy, Barnes said, underlines the importance for a revolutionary workers party today to center its activity in industry and the industrial unions, with its eyes always focused on the ranks—on the young workers, the oppressed nationalities, and women.

The two articles on the aristocracy of labor in this issue of *New International* will be of use to revolutionary workers who are participating through their day-to-day political work in these events and discussions that are changing U.S. politics and foreshadow the coming battles that will lead to the transformation of the labor movement into a powerful class-struggle instrument of the exploited and oppressed.

Other major talks at the August socialist educational conference were presented by Steve Penner, a leader of the Revolutionary Workers League of Canada and an editor of *NI,* on Marxism and the national question; Dodie Ellis, a British member of the United Secretariat of the Fourth International, on the struggle for women's emancipation; and SWP National Chairperson Mary-Alice Waters on the dictatorship of the proletariat as the end result of the social and political struggle of the working class both in North America and worldwide. An article based on the talk by Waters will appear in a forthcoming issue of *New International.* It will be a further contribution to the discussion raised in the article "Their Trotsky and Ours: Communist Continuity Today" by Jack Barnes, published in our first issue.

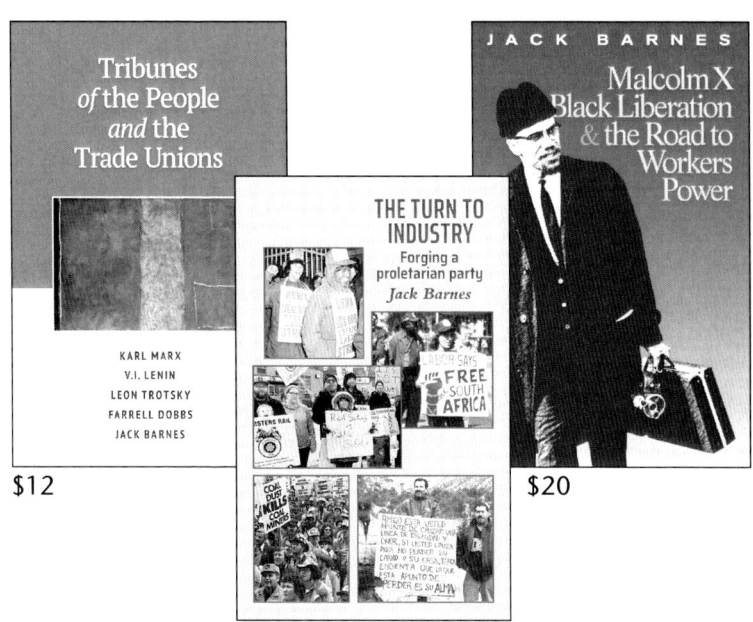

$12 $20

$15

Three books to be read as one . . .

about building a party that's working class in program, composition, and action. One that recognizes, in word and deed, the most revolutionary fact of our time . . .

. . . that working people have the power to create a different world as we act together to defend our own class interests—not those of the privileged classes who exploit our labor, not of those who fear us as "deplorables," or just plain "trash."

As we advance along a revolutionary course toward workers power, we will transform ourselves and awaken to our own worth. Also in Spanish and French.

Special Offer!
All three $30

The Turn to Industry and *Tribunes of the People and the Trade Unions* $20

Either book plus *Malcolm X, Black Liberation, and the Road to Workers Power* $25

WWW.PATHFINDERPRESS.COM

THE WORKING-CLASS FIGHT FOR PEACE

by Brian Grogan

As we meet at this conference, Washington is escalating its war against Nicaragua. The U.S. task force, patrolling a few miles off both the Atlantic and Pacific coasts of that embattled country, is already bigger than that assembled last year by British imperialism for its aggression against Argentina over the Malvinas Islands.

This week the U.S. government is inaugurating what it refers to as a military "exercise" in Honduras. It will be far larger than the Big Pine exercise used as a cover for the attacks into Nicaragua by the *contras* earlier this year. Some 5,500 U.S. troops will be involved inside Honduras, along with a substantial air and naval force.

This massive U.S. military force is not surrounding Nicaragua to carry out war "games." It is there as an essential part of Washington's drive to halt the strengthening and extension of the American socialist revolution. It is there to cripple and, if possible, to overturn the workers

---

Based on a talk given in August 1983 to the Socialist Educational and Activists Conference held in Ohio.

and peasants government in Nicaragua.

These bellicose moves are also aimed at Grenada and Cuba—the other two of the three giants in the Caribbean, where workers and farmers have taken power into their own hands. The toilers of El Salvador and Guatemala—who face full-scale counterrevolutionary wars organized and sustained by U.S. and world imperialism—are also targets of this stepped-up U.S. aggression.

These maneuvers are announced to last for at least six months. In fact, they reflect a qualitative new increase in the direct involvement of U.S. forces in Central America. How long the "exercise" lasts will be decided in struggle.

Meanwhile, the war against Nicaragua being waged by the *contras*—armed, financed, and organized by Washington—continues to escalate. This is daily war of sabotage, subversion, and invasion carried out from bases in Honduras, combined with direct military support from the Honduran armed forces. Let it not go unsaid here that these *contras* state that they are receiving aid from the British government. No class-conscious worker in Britain doubts that the British ruling class, whose hands are already dripping with Argentine and Irish blood, is involved in Reagan's aggression.

The elementary obligation of workers and farmers throughout the world is to join with the Nicaraguans, the Cubans, and the Grenadians to hasten the defeat of Washington and its allies in this war. As they do this, they can confidently endorse the prediction of Ricardo Alarcón, Cuba's vice-minister for foreign affairs, that the imperialists "may be looking for another Beirut, but they are going to find another Hanoi. They will end up fleeing in terror like they did from Saigon."

Already the principled and fearless response by Nicaragua, by Cuba, and by Grenada has slowed down imperialist war plans. The hope in Washington that the show of force, combined with relentless economic pressure, would demoralize and divide the "three giants" has been dashed. Rather it is the bipartisan gang of warmakers in Washington that has been tactically divided, as they weigh the price the class they serve may pay if they use their mighty fleet and Honduran-based troops in a further escalation against Nicaragua.

The stronger, more united, and more intransigent the Cubans, the Grenadians, and the Nicaraguans, the greater the obstacles to imperialist war. So, too, the more intransigent are the workers in the imperialist countries, the greater will be the barriers facing the imperialists in using the military might at the command of their state.

THE CENTER OF WORLD POLITICS today is the battle between the advance of the socialist revolution in Central America and the Caribbean, and the efforts to stop that advance by imperialism, above all U.S. imperialism. That is why the fight against imperialist war today centers on the fight against the war that imperialism is waging against the toilers of Nicaragua, of El Salvador, and their threats to do the same against the people of Grenada and Cuba.

Unconditional struggle against such "colonial wars" is central to the capacity of the politically conscious and organized section of the vanguard of the workers movement in the imperialist countries to advance toward their goals. The fight to transform the unions—the basic and most powerful organizations of our class, embracing millions—into class-struggle instruments is inconceivable without clarity on the need for active and uncompromising opposition to imperialist wars. Our fight is inconceivable without clarity that the "we" that matters is not the workers and bosses of "our" country, versus "them" in other countries. Our interests are those of the toilers everywhere. The "they" we need to fight is the imperialist exploiters of the world—above all the capitalist rulers in our own countries.

The communist course in the fight against imperialist war flows from and is an integral part of the working-class struggle at home against the bosses, against capitalist exploitation and oppression in all its forms. It is an irreplaceable part of advancing the labor movement toward thinking socially and acting politically—independent of the capitalist class, its political parties, and its government. Our antiwar policy is not only inseparable from, but is in fact a tactical corollary of, this revolutionary class-struggle strategy, aimed at bringing a workers and farmers government to power.

Such a perspective can be seriously advanced today only by revolutionary parties based in and oriented to the industrial unions. Only within this framework can we begin the practical work of assembling and educating the vanguard of our class, the work of building a revolutionary workers party. That is why our approach to the fight against imperialist war is also inseparable from the framework of deepening the turn of our parties to the industrial unions, of continuing to transform our parties into organizations made up overwhelmingly of industrial workers.

This turn was the central practical task decided upon by the last World Congress of the Fourth International in November 1979. The report adopted by the World Congress stated, "The sections of the Fourth International must make a radical *turn* to immediately organize to get a large majority of our members and leaders into industry and into industrial unions."

As the report pointed out, "Only parties of industrial workers will be able to withstand the pressures, including the ideological pressures, of the ruling class."[1] Such pressures are intensifying today as the imperialists escalate their wars in Central America and the Caribbean, the Middle East, and elsewhere.

For the working-class vanguard in Britain, as here in the United States, the interrelationship between the turn to industry and the fight against imperialist war is made even clearer by the fact that key sections of the proletariat are made up of workers who came from, or who trace their recent origins to, Africa, the Caribbean, Latin America, Asia, and the Mideast. These workers maintain a special identification with the colonial revolution. There can be no revolutionary perspective in our countries without an orientation to these oppressed sections of the working class.

The revolutionary vanguard must fight for the labor movement to take the lead in combating racist and chauvinist discrimination, demanding positive action (what you here in the United States call affirmative action), and championing other struggles by these fellow working people. They play a vanguard role in the working class, and must become a growing section of the cadre and leadership of our parties if we are to be, in fact, a vanguard of the working class.

The connection between a Marxist course in the fight against imperialist war and the proletarianization of the revolutionary party was stressed time and again by Leon Trotsky in the 1930s, as war preparations and maneuvers by the imperialist powers increased. Trotsky saw the proletarianization of the newly formed Fourth International as essential to tempering and strengthening our organizations so that they would not be disoriented and broken by the increasing war pressure.

In 1938, Trotsky wrote to the U.S. Socialist Workers Party:

> The pre-war situation, the aggravation of nationalism and so on is a natural hindrance to our development and the profound cause of the depression in our ranks. But it must now be underlined that *the more the party is petty-bourgeois in its composition, the more it is dependent upon the changes in the official public opinion. It is a supplementary argument for the necessity for a courageous and active reorientation toward the masses.*[2]

The following year, Trotsky wrote that the SWP "will either become proletarian or it will cease to exist" as a revolutionary party.[3] That remains inescapably true for our entire world movement.

Roots of working-class strategy

Within this framework, the aims of this talk are:

(1) to review and reaffirm the proletarian strategy for the working-class fight against imperialist war;

(2) to look at what is *new* since the time of Marx, Engels, Lenin, and Trotsky that needs to be integrated into this line of march, particularly the importance of the growing consciousness since World War II of the catastrophic destructive capacity of nuclear weapons;

(3) to understand how our strategy prepares us to respond to and participate in united front–type actions,

activities, and organizations in opposition to the wars and nuclear policies of the imperialist ruling classes; and

(4) to explain how building the most powerful fight against imperialist wars in Central America and the Caribbean, the Middle East, and elsewhere, is both advanced by and itself helps to advance the class struggle by workers and their allies in the factories, in the communities of the oppressed nationalities, and around all the broad social and political questions confronting the toilers.

For Marxists, the fight against imperialist war begins from the perspective of leading the working class to a deepening understanding of the class struggle, its forms and character, and its inevitable and necessary outcome—the overthrow of the capitalist rulers and the bringing to power of a workers and farmers government, which will start the construction of socialism. Only with the overthrow of the imperialist powers by the exploited and oppressed will it be possible to begin talking truthfully of building a world without war.

At the same time, with regard to concrete imperialist wars—such as those against the peoples of Indochina, or today against the peoples of Central America and the Caribbean—the mobilization of mass antiwar opposition can become an important political factor in bringing about the defeat of imperialist aggression. Together with the revolutionary war waged by the Vietnamese freedom fighters, for example, the antiwar movement in this country, and the growing political opposition to the war that it gave organized expression to, were important factors that the U.S. ruling class had to weigh in coming to the decision to withdraw U.S. ground troops in 1973. This withdrawal opened the way for the final Vietnamese victory two years later.

In this fundamental sense, the working-class road to

peace is no different from the working-class road to Black self-determination and equality, to women's emancipation, or to ending exploitation and oppression in all its forms. None of these goals can be achieved short of the overthrow of capitalist rule. And communists have no separate strategy for any of them apart from our overall strategy aimed at advancing the class consciousness and organization of the workers and their allies, mobilizing them in struggle against the exploiters, advancing independent working-class political action, combating class collaboration, and so on.

At the same time, demands around all sorts of specific aspects of the oppression and exploitation of Blacks, women, and other working people not only can be won, but the struggle for such demands is an indispensable part of organizing and mobilizing the working class and its allies into a movement that *can* overthrow capitalist rule. So, too, with demands and actions against concrete imperialist wars and war policies.

Based on this understanding, you in the U.S. Socialist Workers Party fought consistently for a working-class orientation in the anti–Vietnam War movement in the 1960s and 1970s. Your eyes were always on how to involve the maximum possible numbers of unions and unionists, Blacks and Latinos, and GIs—workers in uniform. At that time, however, you had to advance this course in a political situation where the labor movement had not yet begun to emerge from the political retreat that had begun in the late 1940s. By and large, you were unable to conduct this political campaign in the labor movement, through the unions, with fractions of your own members in the major industrial unions.

How much better the conditions are for the revolutionary workers movement today, as imperialism escalates its aggression in Central America and the Caribbean. Not only is antiwar opposition much deeper in the working class than it was at the beginning of the Vietnam War, but the worldwide capitalist economic crisis and the changing consciousness and attitudes of workers in face of it can potentially lead to big class battles that will weaken Washington's capacity to conduct wars abroad and win.

OUR STRATEGY in the fight against imperialist war refuses to subordinate the struggles of the workers, of the oppressed nationalities, of women to false notions of "national interest." Instead, it aims at breaking workers free from any collaboration whatsoever with their rulers in advancing imperialist foreign policy aims. The working class must have its own foreign policy, based on forging an international alliance of the workers and the oppressed nations against imperialism.

This means rejecting all attempts to justify class-collaborationism and appeals for "social peace" in wartime. Instead, revolutionary socialists must utilize the effects of the social crisis intensified by the war to lead the workers and farmers as far as possible toward resolving the crisis.

This was the policy followed by the Bolshevik Party in Russia during World War I. The Bolsheviks explained that the Russian toilers had no interest in joining with their oppressors in a war against other imperialist governments over markets and territory—a war that would pit them in battle against fellow workers and farmers from Germany and other countries. Their enemy was at home—the imperialist regime of the tsar. The defeat of Russia's exploiters would be a lesser evil to any subordination of the class interests of the workers there and worldwide to a victory in the war. The Bolsheviks called this policy "revolutionary defeatism."

Rather than join with the tsar, the landlords, and the bosses in pursuing imperialist war aims, the Bolsheviks insisted, the workers movement should seek every opportunity created by wartime conditions to advance *its own* class aims—overthrowing the tsarist regime and replacing it with a government of the workers and peasants. The Bolsheviks summed up this perspective by saying that the strategic aim of the Russian workers movement had to be to "turn the imperialist war into a civil war," that is, into a revolutionary struggle at home against the exploiting classes. This is the only road to end war—the overthrow of the imperialist system which is the cause of war in our epoch.

THE BOLSHEVIKS did not derive this approach to the fight against war from a conjunctural estimate that a revolution was on the immediate agenda in Russia or anywhere else. They derived it from an understanding of the road along which the working class would have to travel to defend its own interests during the war and afterward.

In his 1915 article on "The Collapse of the Second International," Lenin explained that "no socialist has ever guaranteed that this war (and not tomorrow's) will produce a revolution. What we are discussing is the indisputable and fundamental duty of all socialists—that of revealing to the masses the existence of a revolutionary situation, explaining its scope and depth, arousing the proletariat's revolutionary consciousness and revolutionary determination, helping it to go over to revolutionary action, and forming, for that purpose, organisations suited to the revolutionary situation."[4]

The Bolsheviks demanded that this same revolutionary course guide the actions by leaders of all the mass workers parties of the Second International. As Lenin pointed out after the war broke out, these leaders had adopted resolutions at the 1907 World Congress in Stuttgart and the 1912 World Congress in Basel that "spoke, not of 'defence of the fatherland', but of 'hastening the downfall of capitalism', of utilizing the war-created crisis for this purpose, and of the example provided by the Paris Commune. The latter was an instance of a war of nations being turned into a civil war."[5]

When the imperialist slaughter began in August 1914, however, the big majority of leaders of the Second International rallied to support their "own" ruling classes, even joining governments and helping the bosses discipline the workers and repress their struggles.

The Bolsheviks did the opposite. Inside Russia they seized every opportunity, however slight, to educate and to organize workers around issues that clarified what their class interests were and what their goal therefore had to be. When the bosses organized collections in the plants for victims of war, the Bolsheviks organized their own collections. When the bosses cut food supplies, the Bolsheviks demanded that the workers be put in charge of food distribution. When the government set up elected committees to increase production in the war industries, the Bolsheviks campaigned for a boycott of them. And so on.[6]

The correctness of the Bolshevik strategy was confirmed by history. The imperialist war did turn into a civil war in Russia; it turned into a popular revolution that in February 1917 toppled the tsarist regime and in October, under Bolshevik leadership, brought the workers and peasants to power. It was an uprising of sailors, soldiers, and workers across Germany in early November 1918 that finally brought the war to a swift conclusion, toppling the empire and opening up the German revolution. The Bolshevik perspective was confirmed in other countries of Central and Eastern Europe as well, although the workers and peasants in these countries were ultimately crushed by capitalist reaction.

In fact, until the Cuban revolution of 1959, every successful socialist revolution, every overturn of capitalist rule and establishment of the dictatorship of the proletariat, resulted from civil wars of one intensity or another flowing out of imperialist wars and the resulting social dislocation and massive convulsions. This was true not only for the Russian victory following World War I, but—during and after the second world imperialist slaughter—true for the revolution in Yugoslavia, the social overturns in the rest of Eastern Europe, the Chinese revolution, the civil war in Korea, and the initiation of the long national liberation war that eventually swept the imperialists from Indochina.

The fact that victorious anticapitalist revolutions in Cuba, Grenada, and Nicaragua were *not* the product of gigantic, worldwide imperialist bloodlettings registers progress for the proletariat. It reflects imperialism's inability over the past sixty years to overturn the Soviet workers state or to prevent the extension of the socialist revolution to more than a dozen other countries encompassing more than one-third of humanity.

Imperialism vs. workers of the world

The existence of the Soviet workers state is a mighty obstacle to imperialist wars, not a contributing factor to the war danger—much less the main cause of war, as the imperialists try to convince working people. With the overthrow of the Russian capitalist class in October 1917, the Bolshevik-led revolution brought an end to Russian imperialism, and to its inherent drive toward expansionism and war. The establishment of a workers state on Russian soil was a major blow against imperialist war.

It is true, to be sure, that the territory under the dictatorship of the proletariat tends to expand, as the history of this century demonstrates so clearly. This is not a question of "communist expansionism" or "exported revolutions," however, but of the irrepressible upsurge of socialist revolutions, as workers and farmers rebel against imperialist domination and capitalist exploitation and oppression. Every new victory bringing the workers and farmers to power is a step toward completing the process begun by the Russian workers and peasants in October 1917.

The revolutionary upsurge after the first world war extended throughout the Asian territories that had comprised the old tsarist empire, and gave a mighty impulse to revolutions against imperialism and landlord-capitalist domination throughout Asia. The Russian victory failed to extend to Western or Central Europe, however, where the greater size of the proletariat and level of industrial development could have brought decisive economic help to the Soviet Republic, beleaguered by years of civil war and imperialist military intervention. The prolonged isolation of the Russian revolution in the face of imperialist pressures led to the revolution's degeneration, the Stalinization of the Communist parties and Communist International, and a series of defeats of the world workers movement. All this facilitated the spread of capitalist reaction, including the rise of fascism in Europe, culminating in the launching by imperialism of its second world war and the attempt by German imperialism to crush the first—and, at that time, only—workers state.

The Soviet Union emerged victorious from the war against German imperialism, however. This marked a turning point that saw a revival of the international revolution. The isolation of the Soviet Union was broken. Workers states came into being in Eastern Europe. The victory of the Chinese revolution in 1949, the setback to U.S. imperialism's aims in Korea in 1953, and Vietnam's victory over French imperialism two years later, definitively altered the world relationship of class forces in favor of the workers and farmers. The tidal wave of the colonial revolution swept through Africa and the Middle East, and reached a qualitatively new high point with the victory of the Cuban revolution, establishing the first workers state on American territory. In the following years, the revolution triumphed in South Vietnam in 1975, and then in 1979 in Grenada and Nicaragua.

The U.S. imperialists emerged from World War II as the sole possessors of the atomic bomb, which they had used against the Japanese people; they fully intended to use this nuclear monopoly and their mighty armed forces to terrify and where necessary to smash the colonial revolution and prepare for war against the Soviet Union. After the 1945 victories over Germany and Japan, however, the U.S. armed forces proved unreliable for any further immediate war. In the face of protest strikes and huge "Bring Us Home" demonstrations by U.S. GIs, Washington was forced to postpone its plans for a new war. The upsurge in the colonial revolution in Asia and Africa, especially in China, forced back Washington's war plans still more.

Then, to the horror and dismay of the imperialists, the Soviets developed their own atomic bomb by the end of 1949, breaking forever the nuclear monopoly with which Washington had hoped to blackmail the world into accepting its domination. This was followed by the Soviet hydrogen bomb in 1953, and huge strides forward in Soviet rocketry and military capacity, revealing the gains in economic strength as well as advances in science and technology by the workers state.

The power of the Soviet Union's planned economy made it possible for a country that in 1917 had been the most backward imperialist power; that suffered the massive destruction of two world wars, a civil war, and three catastrophic invasions; that has been hampered by bureaucratic mismanagement and totalitarian practices, to nonetheless—within five decades—amass the strength and technological capacity to challenge the might of U.S. imperialism.

The strengthening of the Soviet workers state and the extension of the world revolution from Eastern Europe and China to Vietnam, to Cuba, Nicaragua, and Grenada—all this has qualitatively transformed the world relationship of class forces. Today, it is within this changed international context that revolutionary workers have to approach the question of imperialist war.

FIRST, THE STRENGTH of Soviet military power, including its nuclear deterrent, has dealt a death blow to imperialist dreams of conquering the Soviet Union militarily in any foreseeable time period. Washington had a nuclear monopoly in the late 1940s and a big lead even into the 1950s, but the advance of the world revolution pushed the imperialists back during these years and bought time for the Soviet Union to develop its own nuclear weapons. Since then, the warmakers in Washington have had to recognize that they simply don't have what it takes to attack the Soviet Union militarily and *win*.

Every advance in nuclear technology or missile capability since that time has been aggressively initiated by Washington, but each has been quickly matched by the Soviet Union. The imperialists are condemned to face the fact that a nuclear attack on the Soviet Union would bring their own destruction. A war by imperialism that promises self-destruction loses its purpose, which is victory and greater profits for the victors. Moreover, the people of the United States want no part of a war with the Soviet Union. Even those with the most backward and confused political views are well aware that any attempt by the United States to defeat the USSR in a war would rapidly lead to their own annihilation.

This "Russian syndrome" runs even deeper in the United States than the so-called Vietnam syndrome.

T<small>HE POWER</small> of the Soviet Union has also made it impossible for the imperialists to wage large-scale war against each other, as they did twice during the first half of this century. Despite sharpening interimperialist rivalries and conflicts, the rulers today are unable to resolve the situation by the "normal" method of interimperialist war to redivide the world and force the weaker imperialist powers to submit to the stronger. The workers states would emerge the victor from such a war, which would also pose the direct threat of revolution in one or more imperialist countries and a further massive upsurge of national liberation struggles. In the face of this threat to their world system of exploitation, and despite their rivalries, all the imperialist powers—even those with their own nuclear arms, such as Britain, France, and Israel—rely fundamentally on protection by the strategic nuclear arsenal of U.S. imperialism.

The abolition of capitalism all the way from Eastern Europe to China, and from Vietnam to Cuba, and the growing strength of these planned economies, have forced imperialism to retreat and to refrain from using its nuclear arms.

Thus, the imperialist wars the world has been living through almost nonstop for the last forty years have been neither interimperialist wars, nor head-on assaults against the Soviet Union, but "colonial wars"—wars against national liberation struggles, wars by imperialism to forcibly subjugate the workers and peasants of the colonial and semicolonial world, and wars to attempt to roll back victorious workers and farmers governments in colonial countries. Moreover, the stakes for imperialism have been raised by the fact that their defeat in some of these wars has resulted in big new extensions of the world socialist revolution—in China, in Korea, in Indochina, and in the Caribbean and Central America. Struggles for national liberation in the twentieth century have had an increasing tendency to grow over into socialist revolutions.

The goal of the current imperialist arms buildup, including the nuclear buildup in the United States and in Western Europe, is to give Washington and its allies the freest hand possible to intervene militarily against the colonial revolution, and against the extension of the socialist revolution. This is the immediate purpose of their military encirclement of the Soviet Union with a worldwide network of bases and their massive nuclear arsenal aimed at the USSR. Right now, as we've seen, Central America and the Caribbean are at the center of this international struggle between socialist revolution and capitalist counterrevolution.

The need for workers in the imperialist countries to actively oppose "colonial wars" waged by their own ruling classes is not a new question for the Marxist movement. In a 1916 article, entitled "The Military Programme of the Proletarian Revolution," Lenin sharply polemicized against those in the socialist movement who failed to see this connection between the anti-imperialist struggles in the colonial world and the fight of the workers of the imperialist countries against their own exploiters. He wrote:

> The history of the twentieth century, this century of "unbridled imperialism", is replete with colonial wars. But what we Europeans, the imperialist oppressors of the majority of the world's peoples, with our habitual, despicable European chauvinism, call "colonial wars" are often national wars, or national rebellions of these oppressed peoples. One of the main features of imperialism is that it accelerates capitalist development in the most backward countries, and thereby extends and intensifies the struggle against national oppression. That is a fact, and from it inevitably follows that imperialism must often give rise to national wars.[7]

THIS FEATURE OF WORLD IMPERIALISM is even more decisive today than during Lenin's time. The latter half of the twentieth century certainly has been an epoch of imperialist wars, popular revolutions, national liberation struggles, civil wars, and mass insurrections. Throughout this period, moreover, the working class has increasingly moved to the leadership of the oppressed and exploited in these class battles, thus increasing the chances of their success.

Since World War II the imperialist powers have waged

virtually constant wars to stop the advance of the world revolution. The imperialists intervened against the Chinese revolution. Washington turned the civil war in Korea into a war of imperialist aggression—the first war U.S. imperialism failed to win. The Vietnamese revolution defeated first the French, and then the U.S. occupiers. The imperialists waged war against the people of Indonesia and Malaya.

There have been wars against national liberation movements in Kenya, the Congo, Zimbabwe, Algeria, the African colonies of Portugal, and now Namibia. There have been the British and French intervention in the Suez War, and the series of Israeli wars of expansion, right down to the invasion of Lebanon last year.

The Cuban revolution successfully fought off the counterrevolutionary Bay of Pigs invasion. There have been numerous national rebellions in Latin America, followed by their violent suppression by imperialism, as in the 1965 invasion of the Dominican Republic by the U.S. Marines.

And this is only a very partial list.

Beyond a shadow of a doubt, it is impossible to advance the construction of revolutionary workers parties in the imperialist countries without giving a central place to the struggle to win the labor movement to the fight against the wars imperialism is waging to suppress the struggle for national liberation.

Lenin summed up this interconnection between the struggles for liberation in the oppressed nations and the class battles in the imperialist countries in his 1919 speech to the Congress of Communist Organizations of the Peoples of the East. Because of the transformation of the world that imperialism was bringing about, Lenin stressed that:

> The socialist revolution will not be solely, or chiefly, a struggle of the revolutionary proletarians in each country against their bourgeoisie—no, it will be a struggle of all the imperialist-oppressed colonies and countries, of all dependent countries, against international imperialism.
>
> Characterising the approach of the world socialist revolution in the Party Programme we adopted last March, we said that the civil war of the working people against the imperialists and exploiters in all the advanced countries is beginning to be combined with national wars against international imperialism. That is confirmed by the course of the revolution, and will be more and more confirmed as time goes on. It will be the same in the East.[8]

Today, in continuity with Lenin, we can truthfully say, "It *is* the same in the East and the West"—in Asia, Africa, *and* America and Europe.

Since the rise of imperialism as a worldwide system of capitalist exploitation and oppression, the workers and farmers of *every* country have had a common goal—the overthrow of imperialism. They have had a common world enemy and a common source in the last analysis of their oppression and exploitation—the imperialist ruling classes. This unites the interests of workers and farmers everywhere—in the imperialist countries, in the workers states, and in the colonial and semicolonial world—and advances them along a common line of march toward world socialism.

For revolutionary workers parties in Britain, the United States, and other imperialist countries to ever dismiss wars of national liberation and counterrevolutionary wars against them as merely "local" wars would be to turn our backs not only on the form that imperialist wars take today, but also to turn our backs on the socialist revolution at home and abroad. It would be to turn our backs on the wars by imperialism that can actually push humanity toward a nuclear exchange and mass annihilation.

YET WHAT LENIN REFERRED TO as "our habitual, despicable European chauvinism" all too often warps the views of those claiming to speak for the working class in our countries. We saw this last year when the British imperialists went to war against Argentina over the Malvinas, which the rulers arrogantly called the "Falkland Islands."

Many people calling themselves revolutionaries refused support to Argentina against this massive imperialist onslaught. One example is the *Militant* tendency in the British Labour Party, which calls itself the "Marxist Voice of Labour and Youth" and is one of the many small groups characterized by the British media as "Trotskyist." It opposed British withdrawal from the Malvinas on the spurious grounds that Argentina is governed by a military dictatorship. The *Militant* tendency's criticism of Thatcher was that she did not go all the way and bring down the Argentine government!

Others were "neutral" in the war, indifferent to the outcome of this conflict between an imperialist power and a semicolonial country. They, too, sought to justify their position on the ground that Argentina was ruled by a military regime.

From the *class* standpoint of British workers and the world's toilers, however, the character of the Argentine government was irrelevant to determining what side to take in the war. What *was* relevant is that Argentina is dominated, oppressed, and exploited by imperialism. Our stance was determined by the *objective* needs of advancing the fight to weaken and undermine world imperialism, thus opening the door to advancing the class struggle in Argentina. Lenin fought unceasingly for this approach.

Applying lenin's method in the 1930s, Trotsky wrote an article that is relevant to the debate over the Malvinas. He wrote hypothetically about Brazil, but the parallel is exact to the last letter if we substitute Argentina:

> In Brazil there now reigns a semifascist regime that every revolutionary can only view with hatred. Let us assume, however, that, on the morrow England enters into a conflict with Brazil. I ask you, on whose side of the conflict will the working class be? I will answer for myself personally—in this case I will be on the side of "fascist" Brazil against "democratic" Great Britain.
>
> Why? Because in the conflict between them it will not be a question of democracy or fascism. If England should be victorious, she will put another fascist in Rio de Janeiro and will place double chains on Brazil. If Brazil on the contrary should be victorious, it will give a mighty impulse to national and democratic consciousness of the country and will lead to the overthrow of the Vargas dictatorship.
>
> The defeat of England will at the same time deliver a blow to British imperialism and will give an impulse to the revolutionary movement of the British proletariat. Truly, one must have an empty head to reduce world antagonisms and military

conflicts to the struggle between fascism and democracy. Under all masks, one must know how to distinguish exploiters, slave owners, and robbers!⁹

The Cuban and Nicaraguan leaders showed the world the living force of that approach, as they sought to hug the Argentine dictatorship to death in their proposal to it for an anti-imperialist united front of Latin American countries against the imperialist aggression.

Trotsky sought to bring the lessons of the Comintern to the new generations of revolutionists in the 1930s. He waged a constant battle against sectarian positions within the Trotskyist movement on the colonial revolution, such as those that came up around the Japanese imperialist invasion of China. Like the British sectarians who were "neutral" on the Malvinas war, some ultralefts in the Trotskyist movement in the 1930s were in favor of a position of neutrality in that war. Trotsky wrote in 1937:

> Here the imperialist robbers are engaged in an isolated fight with a semicolonial country in order to transform it into a completely colonial country. The Japanese worker must say: "My exploiters imposed this dishonest war upon me." The Chinese worker must say: "The Japanese robbers imposed this war of defense upon my people. It is my war. But unfortunately the leadership of the war is in bad hands. We must survey its direction severely, and we must prepare to replace it." This is the only real plan for agitation and propaganda.
>
> I have heard the following argument: "The Chinese army is a bourgeois army, but we can support only a proletarian Red army." This argument is a "militarized" expression of the lack

of understanding of the difference between a bourgeois (semi-bourgeois-semifeudal) colonial country and a country of imperialistic slaveholders. As a bourgeois army the Chinese army can of course suppress workers' strikes and peasant rebellions in the interest of the owners. In all these cases we oppose it by all possible means. But in the war against Japan the same army defends— not sufficiently, not conscientiously, etc.—the progressive national interest of the Chinese people. So far we support it. To identify the Chinese army with the Japanese signifies simply identifying the oppressors and the oppressed, the robbers and their victims.[10]

Incidentally, for those who mistook the Cubans' stance toward the Argentine government during the Malvinas war as opportunism or even a touch of Stalinism, Trotsky was talking here about the bourgeois regime headed by Chiang Kai-shek, the same Chiang Kai-shek who had drowned Chinese workers in blood in 1927 and subsequent occasions.

Communists judge our stance on *all* wars today in relation to the worldwide fight against imperialism and for the extension of the dictatorship of the proletariat. This includes wars in which imperialist troops themselves are not openly fighting, such as the current Iran-Iraq war, or the wars in Indochina in 1979.

Why do we support Iran against Iraq in the war that began in 1980? Because the Iraqi regime was the aggressor? No, although it is true that Iraq initiated the war by invading and occupying Iranian territory. We support Iran because the Iraqi aggression advances imperialism's unceasing efforts since the overthrow of the shah in 1979 to weaken the Iranian revolution and liquidate its gains.

Many socialist organizations, starting from the fact that both Iran and Iraq have capitalist governments, refused to back Iran in the war. But the fact that the Iranian army is a bourgeois army and that the Khomeini regime is a bourgeois government doesn't determine our attitude toward Iran in a conflict with imperialism, or in a conflict that helps advance imperialist aims, as the Iraqi aggression does. Nor did our position change when Iranian troops crossed the border into Iraq as part of its defensive effort against the Iraqi intervention and occupation.

Why in 1979 did we support the Vietnamese intervention against the Pol Pot regime in Kampuchea, but oppose the subsequent Chinese invasion of Vietnam?

Because the Vietnamese intervention in Kampuchea was necessary to defeat growing imperialist-backed military pressure against the Vietnamese revolution, and because the overthrow of the Pol Pot tyranny helped extend the socialist revolution in Indochina and consolidate the socialist revolution in Vietnam.

Using the same criteria, we opposed the Peking bureaucracy's invasion of Vietnam because it was carried out in collusion with Washington to intensify the imperialist campaign against the Vietnamese workers state and to hold back the extension of the socialist revolution in Indochina.

Those are the criteria we use to judge all wars in this imperialist epoch.

The connection between the fight against imperialist war abroad and defense of the workers' interests at home was graphically illustrated for us in Britain by a big strike of health workers that was going on when the Malvinas aggression broke out. The Tories issued an appeal for the union to call off the strike in the name of the "Falklands spirit."

These lower-paid workers were not inclined to respond to this appeal, however. Indeed, it is a sign of the limits of the chauvinism whipped up behind the Malvinas War that the typical response was that if money was available for war, then it should also be available for health. But the trade union officialdom, which had fully backed Thatcher's war, was helpless in the face of the Tory appeal, and the union was weakened.

Nowhere is this question more acutely posed for British workers than in relation to Ireland. The fight to transform the unions and the Labour Party into instruments that will fight for the interests of the working class cannot be advanced without unconditional support to the Irish struggle. The fight of the Irish for self-determination is an indispensable ingredient in the fight for socialism in Britain. "A nation which enslaves another can never itself be free," wrote Marx. The dynamic of British politics under the impact of the Irish revolution underscores this point daily.

We are seeing important steps that will help advance this perspective being taken in Ireland today. Last week Gerry Adams, a leader of Sinn Fein, came to London. He was invited by Ken Livingstone, a left Labour Party leader and head of the Greater London Council. In that meeting Adams explained that British workers would not succeed in winning a decisive victory over the British ruling class without supporting the Irish revolution. He also explained that the Irish liberation struggle needs the support of British workers in order to be victorious. He particularly spoke of the common interests of proletarian Irish nationalists and Black workers.[11] This is going to help us broaden the understanding among British workers about proletarian internationalist opposition to imperialist war and all forms of national chauvinism.

The growing debate over imperialist intervention in Central America is deeply affecting the labor movement in Britain, too. A recent labor movement conference in solidarity with Central America attracted more than 300 delegates. They came as delegates from their union or Labour Party constituency, with over half coming from union locals. The largest trade union group was from the coal miners' union, which had every single area and district of the union represented. Tours of Salvadoran unionists have also stimulated interest and discussion within the labor movement.

And from Britain, we have been watching with great interest the tour here in the United States of Alejandro Molina Lara, leader of the Federation of Salvadoran Trade Unions (FENASTRAS), because of what it shows about the changes taking place in the U.S. unions, and the importance of the fight against U.S. intervention in Central America for both our parties' members in the industrial unions.

What a transformation has taken place in the U.S. labor movement! The change is dramatic from a decade or so ago; maybe it looks even more dramatic when viewed from overseas. Molina Lara, a Salvadoran revolutionary union leader, has won a hearing from whole sections of the U.S. union movement, and he has won a sympathetic response from many union members who have heard him. Molina Lara and those who support him in the union movement have even handed a setback to the top AFL-

CIO bureaucrats, who unsuccessfully tried to slap a ban on union invitations to hear him speak.

What is so important about Molina Lara's message? He explains that the Salvadoran union movement, fighting against the U.S.-backed dictatorship there, has common interests with the labor movement here in the United States. He explains who "we" are, and what *we* have in common in our fight against *them*—the U.S. imperialist ruling class and its allies.

As Washington deepens its military aggression in Central America and the Caribbean, as the rulers drag the people of the United States deeper into another war like in Vietnam, the battle inside this country over this war is going to involve higher and higher stakes, and it is going to be even more at the center of class battles. It is because AFL-CIO President Lane Kirkland sees this coming that he has tried so hard to put a stop to Molina Lara's tour, and to intimidate those within the labor movement who defend this Salvadoran unionist's right to speak and who agree with much of what he has to say.

The many industrial workers who are attending this conference this week also see what is coming. You understand that your long-term fight to transform the unions into a movement that battles for workers' interests is impossible without putting the struggle against imperialist war right at the center of your work in the labor movement.

That lesson was certainly driven home to us in Britain by the war in the Malvinas. The imperialist victory was a setback for the British labor movement, a setback that was guaranteed by the chauvinist line of the big majority of union and Labour Party officials, a chauvinism that was parroted even by groups claiming to be socialists, as we have seen. Thatcher emerged from the Malvinas adventure stronger than when she started it.

There is a big difference between what Thatcher was able to accomplish in the South Atlantic and what is facing the U.S. rulers as the Yankee fleet heads toward Central America. The Tory government *won* the war over the Malvinas. And—as wars go—won it on the cheap. The bipartisan gang in Washington knows that it is up against something different, and has good reason to fear that the U.S. government *won't* come out of a Central American war stronger in its ability to maintain stable rule for the exploiters.

Washington's capitalist allies in Western Europe fear this, too. Commenting on the response of European governments to Reagan's latest military moves in Central America and the Caribbean, the *New York Times* reported: "Across Western Europe, a mood of unease began to take hold last week. . . . Particularly in West Germany, there is a sharpening realization that the Reagan administration could hand the free floating anti-missile constituency a new, galvanizing issue if it moves into showdown with Nicaragua or Cuba. The hard core anti-American demonstrators who hurled paving stones and paint filled balloons at Vice-President Bush last month, marched under a banner that proclaimed 'Hands Off Nicaragua.'"

Opposition to nuclear weapons

With the development of the massive destructive power of nuclear weapons since the end of World War II, humanity faces the possibility of an all-out nuclear exchange initiated by imperialism that will end human society. As capitalism develops the forces of production, Marx explained, it increasingly turns them into powerful forces of *destruction,* as well.

Unleashing the strategic nuclear arsenals would not be

a "war" in any sense it has been known until now. There would be no victors or losers, no conquest of territory or peoples, no revolutionary crisis bred by opposition to war. There would only be rapid death and ruin on an unimaginable scale.

It is this reality since the mid-twentieth century that poses the historical alternative before the toilers: either socialist revolution as the road to world peace, or continued imperialist rule, leading to constant wars and eventual nuclear annihilation.

The workers and oppressed peoples of the world will never forget that the first use of nuclear weapons has already occurred—when the U.S. imperialists made the cold-blooded decision in August 1945 to drop atomic bombs on the Japanese cities of Hiroshima and Nagasaki. Nor will people of color forget that the targets the U.S. rulers chose were two defenseless Asian cities. There are few who doubt that those capable of making that decision once are quite capable of doing so again—*if*, as in 1945, they are confident there will be no nuclear retaliation, and *if* they judge that their gains will not be outweighed by the price they pay in horror and hatred by working people at home and around the world.

The development of nuclear weaponry in the thirty-eight years since Hiroshima and Nagasaki has made the workers and farmers throughout the world more aware that the horror unleashed against the Japanese people *could* be unleashed against *them*. So long as there are exploiting classes in power whose interests may require the initiation of a nuclear attack on the proletariat and its conquests, this danger of nuclear annihilation will continue to hang over humanity. Only the overthrow of imperialism will bring an end to that threat.

This consciousness that nuclear weapons pose a threat

to the future of the human race is interlinked with a growing awareness of the danger of nuclear power. Not just nuclear weapons, but the danger of another Three Mile Island, the ever-mounting and insoluble problem of nuclear waste, the threat posed by constant low-level radiation—all have become part of the consciousness of working people in the United States, Britain, and other imperialist countries.

The fact that life-and-death decisions involving nuclear power and weaponry are time and again resolved in favor of protecting profits and plunder contributes to growing distrust in government and big business among broad layers of workers and farmers. More and more working people have come to believe through their own experiences that the capitalist rulers, and those scientists and journalists who do their bidding, have lied about the real dangers of nuclear weapons production and the generation of nuclear energy, covering up the truth to minimize opposition.

THIS CONSCIOUSNESS around the nuclear question, of course, is something new since the writings by Lenin and Trotsky on the fight against imperialist war. Opposition to nuclear weapons and nuclear power provides new opportunities to explain why capitalism offers no future for humanity and to mobilize opposition to ruling-class policies.

We make the demand on the imperialist powers that they halt the production of nuclear weapons and dismantle all those already in place. And we demand a complete shutdown of all their nuclear power plants, whose very existence threatens our life and welfare, and the health of future generations.

Our world movement has sometimes capsulized this position against the imperialists' nuclear arsenal as a demand for "unilateral nuclear disarmament." Of course we understand this to mean unconditional nuclear disarmament. Our point is not that we oppose negotiations between imperialist governments and the Soviet Union for "multilateral" nuclear arms reductions. We would welcome any real progress in that direction. Our point is this: we do not make the demand on our own imperialist government *conditional* on negotiations for reciprocal moves by the Soviet Union, because we hold the capitalist rulers responsible for the buildup of nuclear weapons in the world.

At the same time, there is a political problem with the term "nuclear disarmament" as a characterization of our position. Revolutionary Marxists have always understood that it is utopian to think that any imperialist power can be compelled to "disarm." To raise or support the demand for disarmament simply reinforces this illusion, whereas the task of revolutionists is to explain to workers and their allies that the only way to disarm the capitalists is to take state power out of their hands. As Trotsky put it in the 1938 Transitional Program, "the only disarmament that can avert or end war is the disarmament of the bourgeoisie by the workers."[12]

A QUARTER OF A CENTURY earlier, in charting the revolutionary proletarian course during World War I, Lenin explained that "the disarmament 'demand', or more correctly, the dream of disarmament, is, objectively, nothing but an expression of despair"[13]—despair at pursuing the only course that *can* end war, a victorious revolution against the imperialist ruling classes.

Our demand to dismantle the nuclear arsenals of imperialism is in continuity with, not an exception to, this understanding of the proletarian road to world peace, including the utopian and disorienting character of the demand for disarmament. It is an example of the kind of concrete demands we place on the capitalist rulers around all sorts of questions, aimed at helping to mobilize working-class opposition to their policies and their political rule. While it is utopian to demand "reform" of the cops, for example, it is correct in given situations to demand dissolution of some particularly repressive or murderous unit of the police, or the prosecution of a particular killer cop, or a ban on dumdum bullets.

We explain the cost to the world of imperialism's massive military expenditures. We explain, for example, that the cost of even one nuclear missile could provide the resources to build a whole hospital, or many new schools. We use such propaganda to expose the class priorities of capitalism—billions on new weapons systems, while millions are thrown out of work. Slogans such as "Jobs Not Bombs" link the fight against imperialist war policies to the fight against capitalist austerity, that is, to the fight to sharpen the class struggle against our own ruling classes.

But communists do not advocate "disarming" the bourgeoisie by stages. As the old adage has it: you can't tame a tiger claw by claw. The bourgeoisie will never be persuaded or pressured to disarm. How could it guarantee its continued rule?

Our slogan is that of the Bolsheviks and the revolutionary left wing of the Second International: not one penny, not one man—or woman—for the capitalist war machine! As Trotsky explained to those who thought it more "realistic" to call only for a *cut* in arms expenditure,

"Fifty percent disarmament is the road, not to complete disarmament, but to absolute 100 percent re-armament." Any concession to the "right" of the bourgeoisie to have its military machine will open the working class to chauvinist appeals when the time comes to "defend our country." We are opposed to each and every armament program of the imperialist ruling classes. Not 50 percent opposed, but 100 percent opposed.

Likewise, we stand for the complete abolition of conscription in the imperialist countries, and we fight against its reintroduction where it has been temporarily suspended, as here in the United States. We do not favor a conscript army as somehow "more democratic" or "less effective" than a so-called professional army. A draftee imperialist army is just as "professional," and the rulers need such an army when they go to war for any sustained period. As we know in Britain, moreover, our "professional" army is conscripted on the basis of unemployment, as is the U.S. army.

Today, in Britain, Germany, Holland, Italy, and other imperialist countries, the mass opposition to nuclear weapons is being expressed in demonstrations opposing the introduction of new NATO nuclear missiles, the cruise and Pershing II. In Britain, where the imperialist state has its own nuclear force, most activists in the antimissiles protests, as well as big sections of the labor movement, favor "unilateral British nuclear disarmament." The Labour Party has adopted this "unilateralist" position; so has the miners union, the railworkers union, the steelworkers union, the transport workers union, and others. The determination of a group of women encamped at the Greenham Common military base, where the cruise missiles are scheduled to be sited this fall, has inspired others to mobilize against nuclear weapons.

The mass response to the cry "No to nuclear weapons!" expresses the desire of masses of workers and farmers to rid the planet of nuclear arsenals once and for all. Marxists participate in such actions and recognize their objective role as protests against imperialist policies. We see this progressive consciousness as an important new opportunity to lead working people in the imperialist countries to recognize that the fight against war can only move forward as part of advancing the struggle by the working class against their own capitalist rulers.

In 1963, the Fourth International included this approach in the document—entitled "Dynamics of World Revolution Today"—on which our world movement was reunited after a ten-year split. That resolution said, "In the final analysis only the victory of the proletariat in the most highly developed imperialist countries, above all the victory of the American proletariat, can free mankind definitively from the nightmare of nuclear annihilation." Given this framework, it explained, demands on the imperialist powers that they unconditionally dismantle their nuclear arsenals "can play an extremely progressive role provided that they are linked with other transitional slogans culminating in the working-class struggle for power."[14]

THIS FRAMEWORK IS ESSENTIAL, because demands for nuclear disarmament, including *unilateral* nuclear disarmament, do not necessarily, automatically, or by themselves advance the fight against imperialist war.

Mass movements for peace and disarmament are not a new phenomenon in this century. The mass pacifist sentiment before World War I did not prevent the outbreak of that first world imperialist slaughter. Neither was World

War II held back by the mass peace and disarmament movements of the 1930s, led by the Stalinists and Social Democrats. In each case, these pacifist movements shattered at the outbreak of the war itself, with the majority of leaders lining up behind the ruling class of their own country.

"On the morrow of the blatant protests against war *in general,*" wrote Trotsky in 1934, the "pacifists will scatter in all directions and will not lift a little finger against the *particular* war."[15]

Supporters of our world movement both here in the United States and in Britain participated in the "Ban the Bomb" marches and the protests against atmospheric nuclear weapons testing at the beginnings of the 1960s. But when we brought along signs demanding a halt to the escalating U.S. imperialist military intervention in Vietnam and Laos, the Social Democratic and "third camp" leaders of these demonstrations often tried to exclude us.

A few years later, mass protests began to grow against the U.S. war in Indochina. Here in the United States, the Socialist Workers Party played an important role in mobilizing support for these actions. The SWP fought for a course to orient this antiwar movement towards the kinds of actions and demands that could maximize participation by the labor movement, GIs, and oppressed nationalities and thus mobilize the broadest possible opposition to the imperialist war effort.

Some principled radical pacifists supported this movement, although few if any ever agreed with our proletarian axis, instead emphasizing individual resistance and moral witness. Your main opponents in this movement, however, were various liberals, petty-bourgeois radicals, Social Democrats, and the Communist Party, who sought to channel opposition to the war into support for Democratic Party "dove" politicians, instead of *action* around the clear demand of total and immediate withdrawal of U.S. troops.

As we know, this fight against imperialist aggression in Indochina gave important aid to the Vietnamese freedom fighters in winning that war and contributed to important changes in the political consciousness of U.S. workers—changes that have been important over the past four years as a counterweight to imperialism's escalating military moves against the revolutions in Central America and the Caribbean.

It is an illusion, however, to believe that the imperialist rulers won't go to war in Central America and the Caribbean or elsewhere until and unless they have garnered majority support—an illusion that we need to dispel if we are to advance an effective fight against imperialist wars.

THE RULERS will go to war, and often have gone to war, as a means of *winning* mass backing for military action necessary to advance their class aims. The Thatcher government, for example, judged—correctly, as it turned out—that it could rally more support for its war policies around the Malvinas *after* it sent the massive task force against Argentina than it had been able to marshall beforehand.

The U.S. ruling class followed this course in Indochina. From the beginning of the 1960s it gradually escalated direct U.S. military involvement in the war there, and sought to galvanize popular support on that basis. While the rulers did win some support and acquiescence during the first several years, they were ultimately unable to prevent this majority support from slipping. Mass opposition mounted, contributing to the defeat of the imperialists in Indochina.

This lesson has been confirmed again by the sending of the fleet to Central America, despite mass sentiment against direct U.S. involvement. In his July 26 news conference, after the dispatch of the fleet, Reagan was asked: "Do you have any sense or feeling now for whether the American people are ready to support a war to defend our interests in Central America?" To which he replied: "Well, in the first place, I don't think the American people have ever wanted a war. I think we're probably the most peace-loving people in the world. And maybe this has been part of what has lured us into wars in the past, because we haven't been ready for them."

Leaving aside Reagan's fake "we" and "us," it is true that the people of the United States have never wanted to be involved in an imperialist war, and yet have been dragged into a virtually endless chain of such murderous bloodlettings over the last fifty-five years. This quotation from Reagan's news conference testifies that unless such sentiments are consciously organized along a clear axis of opposition to imperialist wars, even the desire for peace itself can be demagogically used by those who are preparing war—"we" must be well-armed and prepared "to protect peace."

THIS IS VERY MUCH A LIVE QUESTION for opponents of imperialist war today. In Britain, for example, the big majority of Labour Party and union leaders who are on record for Britain's nuclear disarmament at the same time *supported* British imperialism's aggression against Argentina over the Malvinas. Furthermore, most of these officials have done nothing to mobilize working-class opposition to British imperialist complicity with Washington's war moves in Central America and the Caribbean, and the Mideast.

A small handful of Labour Party and trade union leaders did oppose the war against Argentina, indicating the potential to mobilize working-class opposition if any significant wing of the labor officialdom had sought to do so. Opposition to this aggression against a country in the colonial world was particularly deep among the growing numbers of Black workers from the Caribbean and among other Black and Asian workers in Britain. In addition, forces in the Campaign for Nuclear Disarmament (CND) also opposed the war, and there were some modest but important demonstrations while the aggression was under way.

In Britain, support for the demand of unilateral nuclear disarmament can fit in with support for imperialist "national defense"—of the "conventional" variety. In fact, this is the stance of the big majority of Labour Party and union officials who support this demand; it is also the position of the dominant leadership current in the Campaign for Nuclear Disarmament, which argues that possession of nuclear weapons provides no real "defense" for Britain because it means suicide in any nuclear exchange with the Soviet Union.

This opens the door to coupling the call for even British *unilateral* nuclear disarmament with calls for strengthening Britain's *conventional* war-making powers. Again, this is the position of the leadership of the British Labour Party. And the CND National Council recently only narrowly rejected the slogan "Defend Britain Without the Bomb" for the demonstration planned for October 1983 as the culmination of the drive to stop deployment of the Pershing II and cruise missiles.

This approach runs directly counter to the actual class

interests of British workers. What is British "defense"—with or without nuclear weapons? The right to engage in imperialist war "games" against the workers states? To possess armaments to kill thousands of Argentine soldiers in the Malvinas? To join Washington in its war in Central America and the Caribbean? To participate in the imperialist occupation of Beirut? To put down ever more violently the Irish freedom fighters? To smash strikes at home, or to put down rebellions by young Black, Asian, and other workers like those that shook Brixton and Liverpool two years ago?

While it is the worst kind of fakery to spread the utopian illusion that any imperialist government can be "disarmed" short of being overthrown, the existence of the massive U.S. nuclear "umbrella" makes it conceivable for other imperialist powers to forego nuclear weapons of their own while beefing up their "conventional" weapons. Japan and West Germany, to cite just two of the most obvious examples, have no nuclear arsenals of their own.

No wing of the British ruling class today proposes to scrap its nuclear force, since doing so would put Britain in an even weaker position in its competition with its imperialist rivals. But those sections of the Labour Party and union officialdom that advocate British nuclear disarmament *do* in their big majority project this as an alternative "defense" policy for British imperialism. Few, for example, couple this demand with support for British withdrawal from the NATO alliance or support for unconditional dismantling of the U.S. nuclear arsenal.

Working-class politics vs. 'fraudulent abstractions'
Some prominent individuals and political forces associated with opposition to nuclear weapons today argue

that the "atomic era" has rendered out of date the "old" Marxist approach to war—if such an approach ever did have any merit. They claim that the advent of nuclear weapons has changed everything.

The most well-known radical theorizer of this argument is E.P. Thompson, a leading spokesperson for the British Campaign for Nuclear Disarmament. Thompson at one time presented himself as a Marxist, but he has devoted the past several years to propagating the message that the Marxist program and strategy have to be junked, and indeed combated.

Thompson's analysis of the world is based not on the conflict of classes but on his concept of "exterminism"— the notion that the "arms race" has a mad logic of its own, hurtling the world toward nuclear war independent of the national and international class struggle. Nuclear weapons are somehow racing against each other to Armageddon. The "arms race" is "self-generating," Thompson says, not the result of imperialism's drive to defend and extend its worldwide system of exploitation and oppression. Thus, opponents of nuclear weapons should aim their fire equally at the imperialist powers and the Soviet Union since both bear equal responsibility for leading humanity down the path to its annihilation.

Thompson has coined a new word, but the content is merely a current-day rehash of what Trotsky in the Transitional Program called "fraudulent abstractions."

"The bourgeoisie and its agents," Trotsky wrote on the eve of World War II, "use the war question more than any other to deceive the people by means of abstractions, general formulas, lame phraseology: 'neutrality,' 'collective security,' 'arming for the defense of peace,' 'national defense,' 'struggle against fascism,' and so on. All such formulas reduce themselves in the end to the fact that the war question, i.e., the fate of the people, is left in the hands of the imperialists, their governing staffs, their diplomacy, their generals, with all their intrigues and plots against the people.

"The Fourth International rejects with abhorrence all such abstractions. . . . But abhorrence is not enough. It is imperative to help the masses discern, by means of verifying criteria, slogans, and demands, the concrete essence of these fraudulent abstractions."[16]

That remains a task of revolutionary workers today, because these "fraudulent abstractions" do not hover in the realm of ideas. Proponents of such views obstruct the education and mobilization of the working class and its allies against imperialist war. E.P. Thompson, for example, argues that it is "mistaken to argue the case about Central America by trying to attach it to the general issue of nuclear war."[17]

But "the general issue of nuclear war" *is* "attached" not only to the class conflict in Central America, but to the class struggle on a world scale. The struggle against war is an aspect of the struggle against imperialism, of the struggle—as Trotsky put it—to take state power out of "the hands of the imperialists, their governing staffs; their diplomacy, their generals, with all their intrigues and plots against the people." The fight against the imperialists' nuclear arsenal cannot be *advanced* other than by class-struggle methods.

The existence, development, and growth of nuclear weapons stockpiles, while raising the stakes immensely in the fight against imperialist war, do not remove it from the class struggle. Imperialism's nuclear arms buildup—including the scheduled deployment of cruise and Pershing II missiles in Britain and Western Europe—is aimed at making it easier for the capitalist rulers to use their "conventional" military might around the world to pursue their class interests.

Although Washington's vast military encirclement of the USSR shows that it has not given up its historic goal of rolling back the socialist revolution there, the U.S. government and NATO are not gearing up today for a nuclear attack on the Soviet Union. As we've already explained, this is precluded by the existing relationship of forces between imperialism and the Soviet workers state, and between the imperialist rulers and the working class and its allies. Instead, this nuclear buildup is designed to warn Moscow to keep hands off should Washington or its imperialist allies need to escalate their direct military intervention in Central America and the Caribbean, the Mideast, or other fronts of the colonial revolution.

These are the political and military factors that Washington weighed when it slapped the naval blockade around Cuba in October 1962. It figured that the Soviet Union would back down, because of the threat of U.S. nuclear escalation of the conflict. At the same time, the Soviet nuclear arsenal is a major reason why imperialism doesn't simply try to wipe the Cuban workers state off the map.

TODAY, IMPERIALISM'S DETERMINATION to push ahead with its nuclear buildup in Western Europe *cannot* be separated from its determination to halt the extension of the socialist revolution in Central America and the Caribbean.

Reagan in his own way made explicit testimony to this interconnection in his speech to the National Association of Manufacturers on March 10 of this year when he justified the new military buildup in Europe as follows: "Soviet military theorists want to destroy our capacity to resupply Western Europe in case of emergency. They want to tie down our forces on our southern border and so limit our capacity to act in more distant places."

We must not overlook a second way in which the nuclear weapons question is linked to imperialism's colonial wars. Along with the development of their strategic nuclear arsenals aimed at the Soviet Union, the imperialists have also developed "tactical" nuclear weapons that can be used in so-called local wars. Thus the Pentagon's Rapid Deployment Force [RDF], developed as a flexible military task force able to intervene rapidly in the Middle East or elsewhere against a revolutionary insurrection or rebellion, is equipped with its own nuclear weapons. The U.S. has some 17,000 "tactical" or "field" nuclear weapons, some portion of which are available to the RDF. Moreover, the RDF has a wing of twenty-eight B-52H strategic bombers equipped with thermonuclear gravity bombs. Washington has recently begun stockpiling neutron bombs in South Korea—for use there if needs be.

U.S. Secretary of Defense Caspar Weinberger has been quite explicit about how Washington views this question: "It is still possible, I believe, to fight some wars using conventional forces . . . but I think that if you advise potential opponents in advance that you do not intend to cross certain lines, that you have almost assured another Vietnam. . . . Any time you get into a war the possibility that you will use every weapon available has to be left open."

The French imperialist government, too, under the "socialist" government of Mitterrand, has itself developed a 50,000-strong rapid action force, almost identical in conception to the RDF—locked into France's very own nuclear *force de frappe*—ready for use in Africa and elsewhere, as we are concretely seeing today in Chad.

Britain's armed forces can be seen in the same vein, as the Malvinas war showed. It is public knowledge that the British task force in the South Atlantic carried nuclear shells.

Although the Israeli regime has not publicly acknowledged the fact, it too has a nuclear arsenal, and it uses the widespread knowledge of this as powerful blackmail against Arab governments and against the Palestinian people. There is also good reason to believe that the South African regime either has or is close to having its own nuclear weapons.

WASHINGTON'S OPEN THREATS to use nuclear weapons to defeat national liberation struggles is nothing new. U.S. imperialism threatened to use its nuclear arsenal twice during the Korean War, as it did several times against the Vietnamese, in the Taiwan Straits in 1958, during the Cuban missile crisis in 1962, and against Egypt during the 1973 Arab-Israeli war. All these have been made public knowledge by the U.S. rulers, and one can only guess how many other occasions there have been.

There is good reason to point to the danger that imperialism might decide at some point to use nuclear weapons against a national liberation struggle. At the same time, it is important to understand why the imperialists so far have *not* done so. The answer is not identical to why the imperialists have not launched an attack against the Soviet Union, which they are sure could lead to an all-out nuclear exchange. Washington and other nuclear-armed capitalist powers are not at all convinced that all-out war would necessarily result from use of a tactical nuclear weapon against a colonial people.

The main check on the imperialists in this regard is

a political one. Imagine the political price they would pay, for example, for using a nuclear weapon in Africa. Such an act would be met with horror and hatred on a massive scale not only in Africa, but throughout the colonial world, destabilizing neocolonial regimes and risking revolutionary uprisings. Imagine the response in the Black communities of the United States, Britain, and elsewhere, and among other working people in the imperialist countries.

Imagine the political price Washington would pay throughout Latin America and the Caribbean if it were to use nuclear weapons against the peoples of Nicaragua or against Salvadoran freedom fighters. Perhaps we got a little indication last year from the response to the British "conventional" onslaught over the Malvinas. How much greater would be the revulsion and anti-imperialist mobilization in response to the first use of nuclear weapons by an imperialist power against a colonial people fighting for its freedom. Once again, imagine the political price the imperialists would pay at home, in terms of the breakdown of mass confidence in the justice of their rule.

This does not mean that imperialism might not decide at some point to pay such a price. But only if it judged the political costs of not doing so to be weightier than the certain gigantic repercussions of such a decision for the stability of its entire system of rule at home and internationally. Our job is to struggle to keep the political price of any such imperialist use of nuclear weapons high. Every advance by the workers and farmers raises that price; every victory by imperialism lowers it and increases the danger of the use of nuclear weapons.

The insistence on separating the fight to rid the world of nuclear weapons from the class struggle against imperialism at home and abroad is propounded not only by leaders of liberal pacifist movements, such as E.P. Thompson. This line is also advanced by social democratic and Stalinist misleaders in the workers movement. In fact, it is miseducation from this quarter that poses the biggest challenge to revolutionary workers, because these misleaders present such ideas in the labor movement as part of their overall defense of class collaboration with the capitalist rulers.

A<small>LONG THESE LINES</small>, I was particularly struck by the following statement from your own Gus Hall, general secretary of the Communist Party, USA. According to an account in the May 6, 1983, *Daily World,* the threat of nuclear annihilation is so severe, Hall emphasized, "it's almost futile to talk about other things. . . ."

Gus Hall is no pacifist. Nor does he really believe that it is "futile to talk about other things" than the threat of nuclear war. That's not the problem. The problem is what "other things" he wants to talk about, and what he doesn't want to talk about.

What the Communist Party wants to talk about now is mobilizing workers, the unions, and Black and Latino organizations to support Democratic Party candidates— "defeating Reagan at all costs" in 1984. It doesn't want to talk so much about the revolutions in Central America and the Caribbean. Why? Because the CPUSA for decades has pursued a political course that is class-collaborationist in outlook not only with regard to domestic U.S. politics, but world politics as well. In this regard, it models itself on the privileged bureaucratic caste in Moscow.

While the Soviet government justifiably seeks to maintain normal relations with the U.S. government and attempts to negotiate nuclear arms reductions, the conservative bureaucracy holds the reactionary and utopian illusion that such diplomatic deals are the most important way to advance world peace. The bureaucracy rejects the communist position taught by Lenin and the Bolsheviks that it is above all the extension of the world socialist revolution that pushes back the imperialist drive toward war. That is why Moscow today considers steps toward reaching an arms "agreement" with Washington to be far more important than what is happening in Central America and the Caribbean.

In the United States, the CP politically orients to those liberal Democratic Party politicians who it hopes may be most disposed to such a deal, and CP leaders don't want to muddy up this primary goal too much with secondary issues such as intervention in Central America, which could frighten away potential liberal supporters.

That is why Gus Hall says that the nuclear weapons question makes it "almost futile to talk about other things."

Even when CP leaders do talk about opposition to U.S. military moves in Central America, as they do, their aim is not to promote the broadest and most powerful independent, working-class-led opposition to imperialist war moves. Instead, they seek to channel opposition to war into the Democratic Party, reinforcing electoralist illusions. They promote a strategy of class collaboration instead of class struggle. That is why they often find themselves marching to the same tune as liberal bourgeois or petty-bourgeois pacifists, who also reject any strategy based on revolutionary struggle against the imperialist rulers. The same general pattern holds true for the CP in Britain.

Some "left-wing" Social Democratic misleaders in the workers movement pursue a similar course in regard to various antinuclear or antiwar organizations or activities, although for different reasons. They don't take their political cues from the Moscow bureaucracy. They promote class collaboration because it best serves their needs as part of a bureaucratic layer based on the labor movement in their own countries. Like the domestic policy they promote in the unions and reformist labor parties, the foreign policy they advocate is designed to remain safely within the framework of what is acceptable to the bosses and their government.

The last thing that either the Stalinists or Social Democrats consider as the road to peace is any strategy based on independent working-class organization and action, aimed at advancing the workers and their allies along a line of march to the revolutionary conquest of power from the imperialist rulers.

That, however, is exactly the starting point of a Marxist policy for the fight against imperialist war. Right now, building the broadest and most powerful opposition to U.S. intervention in Central America is central to advancing along that road, and for revolutionary workers this requires a course aimed at educating and mobilizing the working class and labor movement to move into the leadership of this fight. Advancing this perspective is impossible without parties whose membership and leadership in their big majority have made a turn to industry and the industrial unions.

Some instructive examples

One instructive example of a tactical application of our strategic approach in the fight against imperialist war is referred to in the *Transitional Program*. This summarizes the position the Socialist Workers Party adopted in 1938, following discussions with Trotsky, on what was known as the Ludlow amendment. In 1935, Representative Louis Ludlow, Democrat from Indiana, introduced a resolution in the House of Representatives to amend the U.S. Constitution to take the war-making powers out of the hands of Congress. The amendment would have required a national referendum before Congress could declare war.

Popular support for this proposal grew, and a campaign around it developed, especially as the rulers began their preparations for another imperialist slaughter. Resolutions endorsing the Ludlow amendment began to be adopted by major trade unions and farmers' organizations. Trotsky urged that the party change its previous line, which had opposed the amendment as simply another expression of pacifist and class-collaborationist politics. He urged the SWP to become "the real champions of the movement" for the Ludlow amendment in the labor and farm movements.

Trotsky explained that what was progressive in the movement was not the illusion that the Ludlow amendment could stop the headlong drive of the rulers to all-out war. Adoption of a constitutional amendment would not do that!

Nonetheless, Trotsky said, the desire of workers and farmers to *wrest the power to make war* away from the capitalist representatives in Congress *was* progressive. In his discussion with SWP leaders, Trotsky explained:

> Now naturally it would be better if we could immediately mobilize the workers and the poor farmers to overthrow democracy and replace it with the dictatorship of the proletariat, which is the only means of avoiding imperialist wars. But we can't do it.
>
> We see that large masses of people are looking

toward democratic means to stop the war. There are two sides to this: one is totally progressive, that is, the will of the masses to stop the war of the imperialists, the lack of confidence in their own representatives. They say: Yes, we sent people to parliament [Congress], but we wish to check them in this important question, which means life and death to millions and millions of Americans. That is a thoroughly progressive step. But with this they connect illusions that they can achieve this aim only by this measure. We criticize this illusion."[18]

I want to stress this, because this is frequently misunderstood about the Ludlow amendment experience. What was progressive in the movement was not any idea that a piece of legislation could stop imperialist war, but the popularization on a mass scale of the idea of taking war-making powers out of the hands of the capitalist politicians. In this context, the popular slogan of the time, "Let the people vote on war," came to mean, "Let the people, not the politicians, have *veto power* over whether or not to go to war." And that helped advance the understanding and mobilization of workers and farmers around the need to take power—war-making power, and all other power—out of the rulers' hands.

SUPPORT BY MARXISTS to amendments to the U.S. Constitution is not necessarily limited to cases where the question of veto power over government decisions is involved. The Equal Rights Amendment, for example, did not involve any decision-making powers; it was a simple statement that no rights shall be abridged on account of sex. Ratification of the ERA would not have ended discrimination against women, of course. But the support for the amendment reflected the growing consciousness among men and women in the labor movement and in broad sections of the population that such discrimination should be barred. The ERA represented an extension of democratic rights. Ratification would have placed women in a stronger position to advance their fight for full equality.

The content of the movement for the Ludlow amendment was the opposite of such campaigns as that being organized today around the ballot measure in San Francisco that has gotten some international publicity lately. This measure reads: "The people of San Francisco call upon the United States government to immediately end all military aid to the government of El Salvador and to withdraw all United States military personnel from that country."

This referendum is a nonbinding expression of opinion, a point stressed by the Democratic Party politicians who are advocating its passage. The *San Francisco Examiner* emphasized this point in reporting on the news conference launching the petition drive. San Francisco Supervisor Harry Britt said, "President Reagan is so completely out of touch with the situation that the only way we can get results is through citizen participation." Supervisor Nancy Walker took a real militant stand: "The waters are very muddy about the issues in El Salvador, but I believe we can make a statement."

In the hands of these capitalist politicians, and those radicals who are promoting their framework, the slogan "Let the people vote on war" has been transformed from its meaning in 1938—to take the war-making power *out of the hands* of Congress—into simply another electoralist scheme in the framework of liberal capitalist politics. Sure, let the people vote—in a nonbinding referendum.

While we send "advisers" to El Salvador and Honduras, and aircraft carriers and battleships to the Nicaraguan coast, let 'em vote. Why not?

In fact, they will let us *vote on everything*, so long as we *decide nothing*. Sure, the rulers say, let the people vote on whether there will be a Democrat or a Republican in the White House. Let the people vote on how much to raise taxes on workers, on whether to have more pollution or more unemployment, on whether you want factories in your city to keep operating. Why not let people vote on war? As long as the rulers *decide*. As long as the workers and farmers have *no veto power*.

THIS PARTICULAR REFERENDUM is just one among many over the past decade, which have in common the idea that fundamental social change can somehow be advanced through an expression of opinion at the ballot. These campaigns take place within the framework of capitalist lesser-evil politics, and they point away from independent working-class political action, organization, and mobilization.

This is not just an issue here in the United States; it is also a question facing the workers movement in Europe. For example, in Italy a "self-managed" referendum is now being carried out by antimissile activists, and presented as a major weapon in the fight against nuclear missiles. And in Britain, the main activity of the Campaign for Nuclear Disarmament (CND) leading up to and during the last general election was a "peace canvass"—a massive opinion gathering effort—that was projected by CND leaders as a major part of the fight against the stationing of U.S. missiles in Britain.

As a political vanguard of the working class, we have

to explain, to clarify, to cut through the fakery of the bourgeois politicians and the confusion spread by petty-bourgeois radicals. We have to find ways to advance and generalize what Trotsky, in connection with the Ludlow amendment, called the "progressive distrust of the exploited toward the exploiters."

One hundred and eight years ago, Frederick Engels put his finger on exactly what we are talking about today in the distinction between the content Trotsky saw in the 1930s movement for the Ludlow amendment and the content the organizers of the San Francisco referendum are imposing on workers in that city who are opposed to U.S. intervention in Central America.

ENGELS SPELLED THIS OUT in an 1875 letter to the German socialist August Bebel. Engels's letter was critical of the program that had been adopted that year at a fusion convention, held in the German city of Gotha, between the followers of Ferdinand Lassalle and the party led by Bebel and Wilhelm Liebknecht. The Lassalleans subordinated activity in the trade unions to electoralism, and they were much taken with the new idea of initiatives and referenda—often referred to as "direct democracy" and "legislation by the people"—that had been first introduced in Switzerland in 1874 and was being peddled by petty-bourgeois radicals.

Engels told Bebel that they had made far too many programmatic concessions to the Lassalleans:

"That a lot of rather confused *purely democratic demands* should figure in the program, of which several are a mere matter of fashion, as for instance, the 'legislation by the people' which exists in Switzerland and does more harm than good if it does anything at all. *Administration* by the people, that would be something."[19]

Administration by the people—wresting *power to decide and implement* from the rulers—that is what the battle is all about. What advances, or helps advance, the workers' fight toward that goal is progressive. What does not is an obstacle.

The task of communists is to shed light on, not to obscure, the line of march of toilers *against* the bosses, their political parties, and their government; to expose the capitalist politicians who talk of peace while preparing for war; and, in line with these goals, to help educate and mobilize the labor movement and its allies in the leadership of the fight against imperialist wars such as that in Central America today.

The campaign around the San Francisco referendum does not advance these goals. It is an obstacle to increasing class consciousness and independent class organization.

Another example of a tactical application of our approach in the fight against imperialist war, in contrast to that of liberals and class-collaborationists, is our stance toward the campaign for a bilateral nuclear freeze, which began in the United States and is now being taken up by leaders of the antimissiles movement in Britain and other imperialist countries. It is true that we would welcome an immediate freeze on any further stockpiling or development of new nuclear weapons by imperialism. Moreover, a bilateral freeze, that is, one negotiated between the Soviet Union and the United States, might also signal a positive step.

The thrust of the political campaign for the bilateral freeze in the imperialist countries, however, is to channel growing opposition to nuclear weapons and government war policies into a class-collaborationist framework that bolsters illusions in imperialist political rule rather than pointing toward independent working-class political action.

The contest for the Democratic Party presidential nomination is making crystal clear what you in the SWP have been explaining about the bilateral freeze campaign since it was launched two years ago. The freeze proposal has become a central plank of most Democratic contenders to enable them to posture as "peace" candidates, as they continue to back the bipartisan escalation of U.S. military intervention against the Central American revolutions and the Pentagon's nuclear and conventional arms buildup. This will continue during the 1984 presidential campaign, whichever Democrat comes out on top.

This, of course, is exactly the kind of thing the bilateral freeze campaign was intended for. The flurry of activity last year around state and local ballot initiatives for the freeze proposal reflected the orientation of its petty-bourgeois radical and liberal supporters toward lesser-evil electoral politics, which forms the bedrock of the capitalist two-party monopoly in the United States. Those currents in the workers movement that joined in the bilateral freeze campaign—such as the Democratic Socialists of America and the Communist Party—did so as part of their overall course toward promoting class collaboration instead of seeking to advance independent working-class political action.

You in the SWP have participated in the discussions around the bilateral freeze proposal in a way that is the opposite from these class-collaborationist currents. You presented the Marxist view on the fight against the imperialist war—the view being outlined here today. You explained Washington's responsibility for the nuclear arms buildup and pointed to the need for a campaign of education and action against the escalating military intervention in Central America. Leading up to the giant June 12, 1982, peace demonstration in New York City—initiated by forces many of whom were also involved in the freeze campaign—you actively participated both directly as a party and as part of the Third World and Progressive Peoples Coalition in the effort to bring the question of Central America, as well as the Israeli siege of Beirut and British aggression against Argentina, into that march.

IN BRITAIN THE FREEZE CAMPAIGN takes a different form due to the existence of the Labour Party, which is based on the trade unions. There, in the wake of the Tory electoral victory in the spring, forces in the leadership of the Campaign for Nuclear Disarmament such as E.P. Thompson have begun to urge the launching of a bilateral freeze campaign as a way of forging an alliance with the forces in and around the capitalist electoral coalition of the Liberal Party and the Social Democratic Party, which was formed by figures who split from the Labour Party officialdom a few years ago. Here again the thrust of the campaign is toward class collaboration and away from any perspective of the independent organization of a working-class fight against imperialist war policies.

Marxists support any genuine fight for immediate demands against the war policies and arms buildup of the bourgeoisie, because such struggles help raise the class consciousness and self-confidence of the working class and advance it along the course toward class independence. As Trotsky put it, we support "every, even insufficient demand, if it can draw the masses into active politics, awaken their criticism, and strengthen their control over the machinations of the bourgeoisie." The bilateral freeze campaign, however, does the exact opposite.

Defense of the workers states

A central reason why the bilateral freeze campaign has won the support of so many liberal capitalist politicians is that it covers up imperialism's responsibility for the nuclear arms buildup. The freeze proposal makes any steps by Washington or London conditional on negotiated mutual steps by the Soviet Union.

This is just one example among many of why an essential part of our task as revolutionary workers is to explain with clarity, from the point of view of the working class, the "Russian question."

Another example is the demand for a European nuclear-free zone from Poland to Portugal. This slogan has been motivated in the following terms in the call for the Second Conference on European Nuclear Disarmament held last May: "We [peace activists 'East and West'] must act together to free the entire territory of Europe from Poland to Portugal, from nuclear weapons, air and submarine bases, and from all institutions engaged in research and manufacture of nuclear weapons. We ask the two super-powers to withdraw all nuclear weapons from European territory."

Some opponents of the U.S. and NATO nuclear buildup have tried to dissociate themselves from this logic but at the same time hold onto the slogan itself. They have argued similarly to those who defend the bilateral freeze. The USSR has no (or very few) nuclear weapons in Eastern Europe now, so the argument goes. Consequently, the weight of this demand is overwhelmingly against NATO, which has large numbers of nuclear weapons concentrated in Western Europe—including the "independent deterrents" in Britain and France. Therefore, the argument runs, the implementation of this demand would actually strengthen the military position of the USSR over NATO.

There are several problems with this approach. The worst error is to invert the real priority of defense of the USSR from the political level to the military-technical one. As Joseph Hansen explained in a 1977 article: "The defense of the workers states occurs on two levels, *political* and *military*. Of these the political is the most important by far." The "political defense of the workers states," Hansen said, "means above all mobilizing popular support."[20]

But the demand for a nuclear-free Europe from Poland to Portugal demobilizes the struggle against imperialism, precisely *because* it blurs the question of who is responsible for the war threat. It confuses precisely the key political point that we must explain.

Moreover, since this slogan holds the "superpowers" equally responsible it does not advance defense of the workers states at the military-technical level either. E.P. Thompson and others have already begun to advance the new slogan for a nuclear-free Europe from the Urals to the Atlantic—that is, including all of European Russia. This demonstrates how politics dominates the military-technical question. We can't explain why the latter slogan is incorrect without explaining points that also apply to the "Poland to Portugal" slogan. Any antiwar policy reliant on tricks or accommodating to the pacifist illusions of the working class will have the opposite of the desired effect.

It is possible to convince a British worker to demand the unconditional dismantling of *Britain's* nuclear weapons without facing squarely the lies built up about the "Soviet threat," since no one believes that the British nuclear missiles would be decisive against the USSR anyway.

It is not possible, however, to convince British workers that the workers of the world would benefit from the unconditional abolition of *Washington's* nuclear weapons so long as they believe the Soviet Union is out to conquer the world and impose a new kind of slavery and oppression on humanity.

This is even more true for workers in the United States. They will never be convinced to demand the destruction of the nuclear arsenal of their own imperialist rulers until they become convinced that *their enemy is at home,* and that it is imperialism, not the Soviet workers state, that is the cause of the threat of war. Without such a revolutionary consciousness, the idea of unconditionally disarming the nuclear arsenal of the United States will never be accepted by more than a handful of moral or religious pacifists.

The imperialist rulers today proclaim themselves partisans of "peace" in the face of Communist aggression. Reagan claims that the U.S. Central American naval task force has been sent to "preserve peace." This is Thatcher's theme as well. The key to peace, they insist, is to contain "Soviet expansionism." All the imperialist governments equally proclaim themselves for "disarmament," but they explain this as the ability to "negotiate from strength." This has been one of Reagan's key arguments for developing the MX missile system, and it is presented by the imperialist governments of Europe as justification for placing the cruise and Pershing II missiles there.

The liberal pacifists, and the petty-bourgeois radicals who often follow their lead, speak in terms of "stopping the arms race" and "universal peace and disarmament." These phrases cover up the fundamental class difference between imperialism and the workers states. They therefore play into the hands of the imperialist warmakers.

The Soviet Union, on the other hand, has no inherent drive toward war and conquest. The USSR has been wrenched out of the imperialist system by the expropriation of the capitalists and landlords. The state exercises a monopoly of foreign trade, and the economy is planned, not dictated by the drive for profits. This historic conquest of the working class has opened the way for giant strides forward for working people.

Okay, some of our co-workers say, this sounds good for Nicaragua or Grenada, maybe even Cuba. But what about the Soviet Union? What is there to defend today?

To this we have to explain that we defend the Soviet workers state, despite the privileged bureaucracy that usurped political power from the workers. The Soviet workers state is diseased, and weakened because of that disease; but it remains a workers state. As Trotsky once put it, the Soviet workers state can be compared to a trade union, which does not cease because of bureaucratic misleadership to be a trade union—an instrument of the workers in the class struggle. A workers state, a far more powerful instrument than a union, does not cease because of bureaucratic deformation to be a workers state—a bastion of the workers both in Russia and internationally.

THIS MARXIST VIEW of the Soviet state has been confirmed by history. Despite the class-collaborationist policies of the Stalinist bureaucracy in Moscow, the Soviet workers state defeated the armed might of imperialism during the Nazi invasion in World War II. Twenty million Soviet citizens laid down their lives in defense of the gains of October.

The course of world history was shaped by this victory in the war. Capitalism was overturned in a series of East

European countries. Popular revolutions triumphed in China and Yugoslavia. The existence of the Soviet Union and these social overturns made possible the victories in Cuba and Vietnam. The existence of these workers states is an essential element of the relationship of class forces in Central America and the Caribbean, and throughout the world, today.

It doesn't take much imagination to predict what the fate, for example, of the Cuban revolution would be if the Soviet workers state were overturned, and capitalism restored there. The Cubans would go down fighting, but they would go down. The relationship of forces on a world scale would be qualitatively changed; the proletariat would be pushed back everywhere, including in the imperialist countries; and the colonial revolution would be dealt a mighty blow. The U.S. government would again use its nuclear weapons when it needed to, as it did against Hiroshima and Nagasaki.

As Trotsky wrote in 1940 in *In Defense of Marxism*:

> The defeat of the USSR in a war with imperialism would signify not solely the liquidation of the bureaucratic dictatorship, but of the planned state economy; and dismemberment of the country into spheres of influence; and a new stabilization of imperialism; and a new weakening of the world proletariat.[21]

The historic ground conquered in 1917 for the working class remains *our* territory, even though it is burdened with a privileged bureaucratic caste that impedes its development, weakens its defense, and pursues policies that place obstacles in the way of the further extension of the revolution.

Trotsky had precise words for those radicals who argued that the workers movement no longer had an interest in defending the Soviet Union because, they said, there was no meaningful difference between the Soviet workers state and imperialism:

> The bourgeoisie appraises this social difference better and more profoundly than do the radical windbags. To be sure, the nationalization of the means of production in one country, and a backward one at that, still does not ensure the building of socialism. But it is capable of furthering the primary requisite of socialism, the planned development of the productive forces.
>
> To turn one's back on the nationalization of the means of production on the ground that in and of itself it does not create the well-being of the masses is tantamount to sentencing a granite foundation to destruction on the ground that it is impossible to live without walls and a roof.
>
> The class conscious worker knows that a successful struggle for complete emancipation is unthinkable without the defense of conquests already gained, however modest they may be. All the more obligatory therefore is the defense of so colossal a conquest as planned economy against restoration of capitalist relations. Those who cannot defend old positions will never conquer new ones.[22]

The bipartisan gang in Washington, like Thatcher and her predecessors, understand this reality—which is why they raise the charge of "Soviet expansionism." The leaders of the British Labour Party answer Thatcher's chatter about the "Soviet menace" by hastily assuring her that they are for "disarmament there too." Naturally, this only puts wind in the sails of the imperialist propaganda.

No better are those liberal pacifists and petty-bourgeois radicals who reply that they support the "independent peace movements East and West." How can you at one moment tell working people in the United States and Britain that they face no "Soviet threat," that they should advocate immediate, unconditional nuclear disarmament of their governments—and then turn around the next moment and tell them to give political support to an independent peace movement in Eastern Europe and the Soviet Union? Any thinking worker would call you a fool or a liar.

FAR FROM HELPING to advance the fight against imperialism's war policies and nuclear buildup, political support for independent peace movements in the workers states undermines the very points on which working people in the imperialist countries must be convinced if they are ever to support the demand for the *unconditional* dismantling of the nuclear arsenals of their own governments.

It is false to claim that workers "East and West" should be united in a common struggle for nuclear disarmament in general, to which the class struggle, including defense of already realized conquests, should be subordinated. Tell that to the Cubans, Grenadians, and Nicaraguans! Tell that to the Soviet workers and farmers!

Yes, workers "East and West" *are* united in a common framework. What unites the interests of the workers and our allies in every country in the world is the fight against imperialism, which is the enemy of all toilers, and for the extension of the proletarian revolution. As Trotsky insisted in 1939:

> We must not lose sight for a single moment of the fact that the question of overthrowing the Soviet bureaucracy is for us subordinate to the question of preserving state property in the means of production in the USSR; that the question of preserving state property in the means of production in the USSR is subordinate for us to the question of the world proletarian revolution.[23]

Pacifist demands of the so-called independent peace movements in Eastern Europe, such as calls on the Soviet Union to give up its nuclear weapons in the face of imperialism, are reactionary—whatever the intentions of some of those who mistakenly raise these demands.

For the same reasons, opposition to the draft in Nicaragua today is reactionary. The decision to begin conscription there (with no exemptions for the clergy, I might add) was greeted with enthusiasm by the workers and peasants when it was announced this past July 19. It is correctly seen by Nicaraguan working people as an essential step in defending Nicaragua against imperialist aggression.

So, too, we hail the appeal by the Cuban government for massive numbers of women to join those already organized in Cuba's Territorial Troop Militia. It is a sign of the vitality of the Cuban revolution, and the advances that women have made in it, that *1.8 million* women have signed up.

In other words, all questions of "militarism" have to be judged in relation to imperialism, to extension of the world socialist revolution, and to the defense of the workers states.

As the 1934 programmatic document, *War and the Fourth International,* put it:

> After the conquest of power, the proletariat itself goes over to the position of the 'defense of the fatherland.' But this formula thenceforward acquires an entirely new historic content. The isolated workers state is not a self-sufficing entity but only a *drill ground for the world revolution.* Defending the USSR, the proletariat defends not national boundaries but a socialist dictatorship temporarily hemmed in by national borders.[24]

Today we can see how Cuba, Nicaragua, and Grenada are more and more the central drill ground for the world revolution. And this approach explained by Trotsky equally describes our attitude in those states governed by bureaucratic castes.

TODAY, WE HEAR ARGUMENTS that all demands in Eastern Europe that involve an "antibureaucratic dynamic" should be supported. But not every demand against the bureaucracies in the workers states is progressive or deserving of our support—any more than every demand against the union bureaucracy, regardless of its content, is progressive. We support the fundamental demands of the Polish workers against the privileged bureaucracy, for example. But the "antibureaucratic" dynamic that the Pope and Polish Catholic hierarchy would like to unleash in Poland is totally reactionary.

The demand by some citizens of the industrially more advanced Croatian region of Yugoslavia that all wealth produced there remain in Croatia, rather than being used in part to develop less advanced regions, is unquestionably aimed against the Yugoslav bureaucracy. But it is a reactionary demand that communists oppose, and a movement supporting such a demand is reactionary.

The pacifist demands of the "independent peace movements" in the Eastern European workers states are *not* a progressive alternative to the policies of the ruling bureaucracies, nor is any movement fighting for such demands progressive merely because it is opposed to these bureaucracies.

The only "antibureaucratic dynamic" that is in the interests of the working class in these countries or worldwide is one that strengthens and advances the workers state, and this necessarily excludes movements for demands that weaken the defense of the workers states.

Our indictment of the bureaucratic castes is not that they arm the workers states against imperialism, implement conscription, or carry on military training of young people. Our criticism is of the class-collaborationist course followed by these bureaucrats, which is an obstacle to the fight against imperialism and imperialist war and the defense and progress of the workers states. Why don't they follow the example of the revolutionary leadership of the Cuban workers state by educating and mobilizing working people in the spirit of militant internationalist solidarity with struggle by the oppressed and exploited around the world? Why are young people not imbued, as they are in Cuba, with the desire to go abroad to serve as internationalist volunteers at the service of the world revolution?

While welcoming any positive diplomatic initiatives taken by the Soviet government on the nuclear arms question, such as those by Premier Andropov earlier this year, we at the same time recognize that the bureaucrats' reliance on diplomatic deals with imperialism, to which they subordinate independent working-class mobilization and struggle, hinders them from taking the kind of bold political initiatives that could promote working-class opposition to the imperialists and win praise and admiration for the Soviet Union by class-conscious workers around the world.

These are the lines along which a communist vanguard of the working class will develop in Eastern Europe and the Soviet Union capable of offering an alternative political course and to sweep aside the bureaucratic misleaders and permit the advance of these workers states as part of the extension of the world revolution against imperialism.

Of course, as the working class in these countries tries to find its way to an alternative political course, including an internationalist fight against imperialist war, there are bound to be confused and contradictory ideas. We don't consider such workers to be counterrevolutionaries, although reactionary elements from the church and other milieus do try to exploit such confusion and will succeed in some instances. Nor do we advocate suppression of the right to express these incorrect views.

But our responsibility toward the working class of these countries is to fight for clarity, not to adapt to wrong and even reactionary ideas. Our fire is directed against those who—in the name of Marxism—adapt to and endorse these confusions, and therefore themselves become part of the obstacle that these workers must surmount in their fight for political clarity on the centrality of the battle against imperialism, which is at the heart of their own political tasks and strategy.

One thing is certain: workers on any mass scale in Eastern Europe and the Soviet Union will *never* respond to such pacifist appeals for disarmament in the face of the massive imperialist threat they face and their collective historical memories of World War II and the imperialist invasion of 1918–20.

OUR TASK in the bureaucratized workers states in Eastern Europe and the Soviet Union is to gather the initial cadres of a political current that roots itself firmly in the continuity of the October 1917 revolution and its Bolshevik leadership; a cadre that clearly understands that Stalin's policies represented the negation of Lenin's; a cadre that charts a domestic and international course like that of the Cubans and Nicaraguans, instead of that of the privileged bureaucracies, the social democratic misleaders, and centrist currents. We don't advance toward that goal one iota by adapting to confused and reactionary ideas that emerge among dissident currents in the bureaucratized workers states.

A real alternative to the class-collaborationist "peace" program of the Stalinist castes was spelled out by Fidel Castro in the course of his 1968 speech on the Warsaw Pact invasion of Czechoslovakia:

> The real promoters of war, the real adventurers, are the imperialists. Now, then, these dangers are real, they are a reality. And this reality cannot be changed by simply preaching, in one's own house, an excessive desire for peace. In any case, the preaching should be done in the enemy's camp and not in one's own camp, because this would only contribute to stifling militancy, to weakening the peoples' readiness to face the risks, sacrifices, not only the possible ultimate sacrifice of one's own life, but also material sacrifice.

> And when the peoples know that the realities of the world, the independence of the country, and the internationalist duties demand investment and sacrifices in the strengthening of the defense of the country, the masses are much better prepared to work with enthusiasm to achieve this, to make sacrifices; understanding this need, being conscious of the dangers that arise when the people have been stirred up and softened by a consistent, foolish and inexplicable campaign in favor of peace. It is a very strange way of demanding peace. That is why we who at the beginning did so many foolish things out of ignorance or naïveté, for a long time now have not painted any signs around here saying "Long Live Peace," "Long Live This," "Long Live That."
>
> Because at the beginning, out of mimicry, by imitation we repeated things as they arrived here, until we reached a point, well, what is the meaning of "Long Live Peace"? Let's put up that sign in New York: "Long Live Peace" in New York, "Long Live Peace" in Washington.[25]

This is the way to educate the youth in East Germany who raise the slogan, "Melt down the weapons," or the East German women who oppose the introduction of military education into high school curricula and conscription of women.

The class-struggle road

There are no greater cynics and hypocrites than those liberals and class-collaborationists today who solemnly pledge themselves to "world peace," while refusing to lead the workers in action against the *war* that the U.S.

rulers today are waging in Central America and the Caribbean.

As Fidel Castro indicated in the above-cited speech, peace will not be brought closer by asking the oppressed of the world to postpone their battles for liberation from imperialism because the world situation is too "dangerous." The demand for peace has to be aimed against the imperialists, who use massive violence to repress the struggles of the oppressed and exploited for national liberation and a just social order.

To those who counsel retreat before imperialism—in the name of "peace"—the revolutionary leaders of the struggles in Central America and the Caribbean respond that slowing down their struggle will not advance that cause. Every advance for the revolution in Central America and the Caribbean today deals a blow to the imperialist warmakers; every defeat, on the other hand, emboldens them.

This does not mean that revolutionists relish war and bloodshed. To the contrary. The Sandinistas, the New Jewel Movement, and the Cuban Communist Party have all continually expressed their desire and readiness to negotiate with Washington. The Farabundo Martí National Liberation Front and Revolutionary Democratic Front in El Salvador have also repeatedly called for "dialogue" with the imperialist power. Washington, however, rejects serious talks.

At the same time, these revolutionists have all refused to surrender their sovereignty or pull back from struggle under Reagan's threats and military pressures. If anything can force the imperialists to the negotiating table, they understand, it will be further advances by the revolutionary forces, not a display of weakness and irresolution. That is how the Vietnamese forced Washington to sit down and talk, leading to the 1973 Paris Peace Accords and the withdrawal of U.S. ground troops from Indochina.

As FIDEL CASTRO EXPLAINED this July 26, the thirtieth anniversary of the assault on the Moncada barracks:

> Just a year has passed since a NATO country [Britain], supported by the United States, waged war on a Latin American nation [Argentina], constituting an affront and a humiliation to the peoples in Our America. Now the United States, in a call to battle stations, is advancing its squadrons and troops in a threatening fashion against another Latin American nation. A new Vietnam in the heart of the American continent? May it never happen, and there's still time to avoid it! The peoples of Our America and the rest of the world would not sit back and observe a crime of such magnitude.
> The same aggressive policy of the present U.S. administration is found everywhere in the world: in the Middle East, southern Africa, in the Indian Ocean, and even in Europe, where the deployment of 572 medium-range strategic nuclear missiles is scheduled to take place soon. . . .
> We are living in risky and difficult times. The threat of confrontation is not only local; it is worldwide. We need nerves of steel, the greatest strength, the greatest mobilization of the peoples, and an absolute determination not to yield to blackmail if we are to stop the aggressor, if we are to safeguard peace, if we are to survive.[26]

The FSLN, too, is providing an inspiring example of

the anti-imperialist fight for peace. Commander Daniel Ortega explained in a speech to the Nicaraguan Territorial Militia, also given July 26:

> We are internationalists. . . . We know that in this struggle, a struggle in which we have the fundamental responsibility to resist and win, not only will brothers from Latin America and other parts of the world come here to our country to fight imperialism. We are also certain that they will step up the protests, the struggles, that are already underway in their own homelands, in their own countries, against these steps toward war by our enemies.
>
> The U.S. warmakers should not for a moment think that if they intervene against us, that it is only here that they will receive the justice of bullets. We are certain that once they intervene against us, throughout Latin America, wherever the warmakers, those who intervene, have representatives, the peoples of Latin America will also make them feel the weight of justice of our Latin America.
>
> The warmakers should not for a moment think that things will remain peaceful for them while they bomb our children, while they bomb our people. We are also certain that from among the people of the United States itself there will surge forward efforts of solidarity and justice against this intervention.
>
> We want to reaffirm our decision to press forward with our revolutionary process, our decision not to yield before these threats, before these military maneuvers, before this escalation that is being carried out daily at our borders. We

have decided to continue preparing ourselves in defense, to resist the blockade, and to resist and defeat the intervention. And this intervention, we know how to confront it, not only in our territory but also wherever the invaders come from. They should not for a moment think that in case of intervention, only our country will be destroyed.

These statements by Castro and Ortega call to mind Lenin's statement in 1906, when he was still expecting an intensification of the mass revolutionary struggle that had begun the previous year in Russia, that, "Contempt for death must become widespread . . . and will ensure victory."[27]

The hatred of imperialism by the workers and peasants of Central America and around the world is a profoundly revolutionary factor in today's world. This hatred, particularly of the U.S. ruling class—the most powerful ruling class and the only one ever to use nuclear weapons—has been deepened by the understanding of the terrible consequences that follow from any use of nuclear warheads.

But hatred of imperialism is not the same thing as *fear*. Fear of imperialism is not progressive, and political strategies tailored to fear can only lead to class-collaborationist conclusions. That is what liberal pacifists and reformist misleaders of our class try to appeal to when they seek to separate opposition to nuclear weapons from the fight against imperialist war.

In imperialist countries such as the United States and Britain, what Trotsky called the "pacifism of the masses," that is, the hatred of war by working people, can become transformed into hatred for the exploiters, into identification with those who are standing up and fighting against imperialism, and into understanding that the power to make war must be wrested from the hands of the capitalist ruling class.

BUT FEAR THAT WEAKENS AND PARALYZES, fear that our class enemy is all-powerful, that the world is doomed, that future generations will never be born—the fear that grows into terrified *inaction,* not confident *action*—is an obstacle to fighting imperialism.

Fidel Castro put it this way in 1981:

> Many may ask themselves if we are living the end of a stage or a final stage. Will mankind survive, we could all ask ourselves.
>
> For the first time in human society, man is confronted by these dramatic concerns. We must face these real dangers serenely and courageously. We cannot afford to be pessimistic, for then the battle for peace would be lost beforehand. We cannot be cowardly, for then dignity as well as peace would be lost beforehand. We can and should preserve peace without yielding an inch, backed by the mobilization of the peoples, including the U.S. people, and by the immense power of opinion and of universal consciousness, as shown during Vietnam's heroic struggle; by the current balance of forces between socialism and imperialism, which the latter vainly seeks to tilt in its favor; by the peoples' capacity and decision to struggle so as to resist any imperialist aggression; by international solidarity which can be expressed in a thousand different ways.
>
> We trust even the imperialists' spirit of self-

preservation, who know that if nuclear war breaks out, they too will unavoidably be turned to ashes.

We will save peace if its enemies know that we are prepared to die for it rather than yield to blackmail and fear![28]

The imperialists and their mouthpieces consciously seek to use the fear of nuclear annihilation to advance their own reactionary aims.

They use it to increase fear of the Soviet Union, a nuclear-armed state, thus diverting the focus from the real source of war.

They use fear of their own nuclear arsenal to try to intimidate the oppressed and exploited of the world, to compel them to accept the continuation of imperialist rule.

They promote the idea that revolutionary struggles bring the world closer to "the brink." This can only lead to the view that the oppressed and exploited should trim their sails in order not to "provoke" the imperialists.

It is false and reactionary ideas such as these that Gus Hall is promoting when he says, given the existence of nuclear weapons, that it is "futile to talk about other things."

The true communist policy, in contrast, always focuses attention on the "other things," as the only way *to prevent* nuclear destruction at the hands of the imperialists. It will be the increasing political organization of the working class in the mines, mills, and factories, in the communities of the oppressed nationalities, and on every front of the battle against exploitation and oppression that will also push back the rulers' capacity to wage war.

Who will be the leaders of these battles? The working class. The workers in the bastions of industry and the industrial unions. The most oppressed layers of the working class. The young workers. The workers from the oppressed nationalities. The immigrant workers. The women workers.

The fight for a class-struggle leadership of our class and its unions, and the fight for working-class leadership of the struggles of all the oppressed and exploited—this is also the fight for a revolutionary leadership of the fight against imperialist war. It will come from nowhere else.

The fight to transform the unions into revolutionary instruments, the fight for independent labor political action, the fight against imperialist war and nuclear weapons—these are all aspects of the same fight. This can be hard to see at the current juncture of the class struggle, when the political radicalization of the working class is still just beginning and the class-collaborationist misleaders maintain their grip on the labor movement. But it is along this common course that these struggles will advance and ultimately triumph. The only road to ending imperialist war is a class-struggle course toward taking state power from the imperialists and establishing a workers and farmers government.

THAT IS WHY our turn to industry and our conscious efforts to proletarianize our parties are inseparably connected to our course in combatting wars and the nuclear buildup by the bourgeoisie. It flows from our working-class program and strategic orientation. Once we're clear on that, then all sorts of tactical questions relating to meetings, demonstrations, coalitions, or whatever become much more straightforward. As a nucleus of revolutionary workers, we seek to take advantage of any opportunity—whether or not it originates inside the labor movement at this point—to advance our class and its allies along this line of march.

It is this perspective that we seek to advance through our industrial fractions and branches in helping to get Salvadoran union leaders before as many union audiences as possible. In our unions, in Black and Latino organizations, and in women's rights groups, we put forward the need to become actively involved in opposing U.S. policy in Central America and the massive government arms budget, including weapons for mass annihilation.

In action coalitions or organizations formed around opposition to U.S. intervention or nuclear weapons, we stress the need to involve labor and the organizations of oppressed nationalities and women. We set priorities and make tactical judgements about particular conferences, demonstrations, and initiatives for action based on our judgement of how best to take another step in this overall direction under the given circumstances.

Lenin said that "the experience of war . . . stuns and breaks some people, *but enlightens and tempers others.*"[29]

In the last analysis, there are two "roads to peace." Those who are stunned and broken by war, who surrender to the exploiters under its pressure, end up with what Sandinista leader Daniel Ortega has called the "peace of the tomb."[30] Given imperialism's massive nuclear arsenal, the tomb today could be that of all humanity.

But we are confident from the record of the working class over this century that the oppressed and exploited are marching along the other road—that of revolutionary class struggle against imperialism. It is the road along which the workers and peasants of Central America and the Caribbean are marching. The road that has led to victories over imperialism from Russia to Vietnam, from countries as gigantic as China to islands as small as Grenada. And it is the road into which feed the struggles by workers, farmers, and the oppressed in the United States, Britain, and other imperialist countries.

There have been many wars along the way, and there will be many others before the end of that road is reached—before the final victory over imperialism opens the way to the construction of world socialism. But that is the *only* road that leads to world peace, and it is only those who are enlightened and tempered by the inevitable wars along the way, rather than stunned and broken by them, who can help ensure the defeat of the exploiters and point the way toward a world without war.

We are determined to do our best to be part of building the kind of revolutionary working-class leadership, in our own countries and on an international scale, that can measure up to that task.

NOTES

1. Jack Barnes, "The Turn to Industry and the Tasks of the Fourth International," in *1979 World Congress of the Fourth International* (New York: *Intercontinental Press*, 1980), p. 44.

2. Leon Trotsky, *In Defense of Marxism* (New York: Pathfinder Press, 1973), p. 113.

3. Ibid., p. 94.

4. V.I. Lenin, "The Collapse of the Second International," in Lenin, *Collected Works* (hereinafter referred to as *CW*) (Moscow: Progress Publishers, 1974), vol. 21, pp. 216–17.

5. Lenin, "The Position and Tasks of the Socialist International," in Lenin, *CW*, vol. 21, p. 39.

6. For a participant's account of these events, see Alexander Shlyapnikov, *On the Eve of 1917* (London: Allison and Busby, 1982).

7. Lenin, "The Military Programme of the Proletarian Revolution," in Lenin, *CW*, vol. 23, p. 78.

8. Lenin, "Address to the Second All-Russia Congress of Communist Organisations of the Peoples of the East, November 22, 1919," in Lenin, *CW*, vol. 30, p. 159.

9. Leon Trotsky, "Anti-Imperialist Struggle is the Key to Liberation," in *Writings of Leon Trotsky, 1938–39* (New York: Pathfinder Press, 1974), p. 34.

10. Leon Trotsky, "Concerning the Resolution on the War," in *Leon Trotsky on China* (New York: Monad Press, 1976), p. 575.

11. Gerry Adams, "Irish Fighter Appeals to British Workers," *Intercontinental Press* (October 3, 1983), pp. 542–43.

12. Leon Trotsky, "The Death Agony of Capitalism and the Tasks of the Fourth International," in Trotsky, *The Transitional Program for Socialist Revolution* (New York: Pathfinder Press, 1977), p. 129.

13. V.I. Lenin, "The 'Disarmament' Slogan," in Lenin, *CW*, vol. 23, p. 96.

14. "Dynamics of World Revolution Today," in *Dynamics of World Revolution Today* (New York: Pathfinder Press, 1974), p. 61.

15. Leon Trotsky, "War and the Fourth International," in *Writings of Leon Trotsky, 1933–34* (New York: Pathfinder Press, 1975), p. 318.

16. Leon Trotsky, "The Death Agony of Capitalism and the Tasks of the Fourth International," in *The Transitional Program*, pp. 128–29.

17. E.P. Thompson, in "Solomon-Thompson Letters II," *The Nation* (June 11, 1983), p. 736.

18. Leon Trotsky, "The Struggle Against War, and the Ludlow Amendment," in *The Transitional Program*, p. 93.

19. Frederick Engels, letter to August Bebel of March 18–28, 1875, in *Marx-Engels Selected Correspondence* (Moscow: Progress

Publishers, 1975), p. 275. Emphasis in original.

20. Morris Starsky and Joseph Hansen, "Concerning the Defense of the Soviet Union: Comment," *Intercontinental Press* (July 4, 1977), p. 774.

21. Trotsky, *In Defense of Marxism*, p. 122.

22. Leon Trotsky, "Manifesto of the Fourth International on the Imperialist War and the Proletarian World Revolution," in *Writings of Leon Trotsky, 1939–40* (New York: Pathfinder Press, 1973), p. 199.

23. Trotsky, *In Defense of Marxism*, p. 21.

24. Trotsky, "War and the Fourth International," p. 312.

25. Fidel Castro, "On the Soviet Occupation of Czechoslovakia," in *Selected Speeches of Fidel Castro* (New York: National Education Department, Socialist Workers Party, 1979), p. 113.

26. Fidel Castro, "Our People are Prepared to Resist Aggression," *Intercontinental Press* (September 5, 1983), p. 487.

27. V.I. Lenin, "Lessons of the Moscow Uprising," in Lenin, *CW*, vol. 11, p. 178.

28. Fidel Castro, "The Crisis of World Capitalism," *Intercontinental Press* (November 2, 1981), p. 1079.

29. Lenin, "The Collapse of the Second International," p. 216.

30. Daniel Ortega, "We Must Prepare to Fight and Win," *Intercontinental Press* (August 8, 1983), p. 440.

CAPITALIST CRISIS AND THE FIGHT FOR WORKERS POWER

Are They Rich Because They're Smart?
Class, Privilege, and Learning under Capitalism

JACK BARNES

Exposes growing class inequalities in the US and the self-serving rationalizations of well-paid professionals who think their "brilliance" equips them to "regulate" working people, who don't know what's in their own best interest. $10. Also in Spanish, French, Farsi, and Arabic.

The Clintons' Anti-Working-Class Record
Why Washington Fears Working People

JACK BARNES

What working people need to know about the profit-driven course of Democrats and Republicans alike over the last three decades. And the political awakening of workers seeking to understand and resist the capitalist rulers' assaults. $10. Also in Spanish, French, Farsi, and Greek.

The Transitional Program for Socialist Revolution
LEON TROTSKY

The Socialist Workers Party program, drafted by Trotsky in 1938, still guides the SWP and communists the world over. The party "uncompromisingly gives battle to all political groupings tied to the apron strings of the bourgeoisie. Its task—the abolition of capitalism's domination. Its aim—socialism. Its method—the proletarian revolution." $17. Also in Farsi.

In Defense of the US Working Class
MARY-ALICE WATERS

Drawing on the fighting traditions of the oppressed and exploited of all colors and national origins, in 2018 tens of thousands of teachers and other working people in West Virginia, Oklahoma, and other states waged victorious strikes. They fought for dignity and respect for themselves, their families, and for all working people. $7. Also in Spanish, French, Farsi, and Greek.

Is Socialist Revolution in the US Possible?
A Necessary Debate among Working People
MARY-ALICE WATERS

Fighting for a society only working people can create, it is our own capacities we will discover. And along that course we will answer the question posed here with a resounding "Yes." Possible but not inevitable. That depends on us. $7. Also in Spanish, French, and Farsi.

"It's the Poor Who Face the Savagery of the US 'Justice' System"
The Cuban Five Talk about Their Lives within the US Working Class

How US cops, courts, and prisons work as "an enormous machine for grinding people up." Five Cuban revolutionaries framed up and held in US jails for 16 years explain the human devastation of capitalist "justice"—and how socialist Cuba is different. $10. Also in Spanish, Farsi, and Greek.

WWW.PATHFINDERPRESS.COM

THE RUSSIAN REVOLUTION

Lenin's Final Fight
Speeches and Writings, 1922–23
V.I. LENIN

In 1922 and 1923, V.I. Lenin, central leader of the world's first socialist revolution, waged what was to be his last political battle—one that was lost following his death. At stake was whether that revolution, and the international communist movement it led, would remain on the proletarian revolutionary course that had brought workers and peasants to power in October 1917. $17. Also in Spanish, Farsi, and Greek.

In Defense of Marxism
Against the Petty-Bourgeois Opposition in the Socialist Workers Party
LEON TROTSKY

A reply to those in the revolutionary workers movement in the late 1930s bending to bourgeois patriotism during Washington's buildup to enter World War II. Trotsky explains why only a party fighting to bring workers into its ranks and leadership can steer a communist course. In the process, he defends the materialist and dialectical foundations of Marxism. $17. Also in Spanish.

The Communist Manifesto
KARL MARX AND FREDERICK ENGELS

Communism, say the founding leaders of the revolutionary workers movement, is not a set of ideas or preconceived "principles" but workers' line of march to power, springing from a "movement going on under our very eyes." $5. Also in Spanish, French, Farsi, and Arabic.

The History of the Russian Revolution

LEON TROTSKY

How, under Lenin's leadership, the Bolshevik Party led millions of workers and farmers to overthrow the state power of the landlords and capitalists in 1917 and bring to power a government that advanced their class interests at home and worldwide. Unabridged, 3 vols. in one. Written by one of the central leaders of that socialist revolution. $30. Also in French and Russian.

To See the Dawn

Baku, 1920—First Congress of the Peoples of the East

How can peasants and workers in the colonial world achieve freedom from imperialist exploitation? By what means can working people overcome divisions incited by their national ruling classes and act together for their common class interests? These questions were addressed by 2,000 delegates to the 1920 Congress of the Peoples of the East. $17

The Revolution Betrayed

What Is the Soviet Union and Where Is It Going?

LEON TROTSKY

In 1917 workers and peasants of Russia were the motor force for one of the deepest revolutions in history. Yet within ten years a political counterrevolution by a privileged social layer, whose chief spokesperson was Joseph Stalin, was being consolidated. The classic study of the Soviet workers state and its degeneration. $17. Also in Spanish, Farsi, and Greek.

WWW.PATHFINDERPRESS.COM

THE DEVELOPMENT OF THE MARXIST POSITION ON THE ARISTOCRACY OF LABOR

by Steve Clark

IN THIS ISSUE of *New International* we are printing a translation of major excerpts from a 1916 article on "The Social Roots of Opportunism" by Gregory Zinoviev, a central leader of the Bolshevik Party and of the early Communist International. It was written in Russian by Zinoviev as a chapter of a planned book, entitled *The War and the Crisis of Social Democracy*. The manuscript was suppressed by the tsarist censors, however, and the book did not appear until after the victory of the October 1917 revolution in Russia.

The article was written during a period when Zinoviev was in daily political collaboration with Bolshevik leader V.I. Lenin. Both were living in forced exile in Switzerland, where they edited and wrote for the official Bolshevik newspaper, *Sotsial-Demokrat,* and coordinated the work of the Bolshevik Party leadership in exile. Lenin and Zinoviev collaborated in drafting many of the party's major statements on political questions during World War I. These included the 1915 article "Socialism and War: The Attitude of the R.S.D.L.P. Towards the War," as well as a collection of articles published in

1918 under the title *Against the Stream*.

The outbreak of World War I in August 1914 dealt a shattering blow to the principal international organization of the workers movement, the Second International. At its 1907 world congress in Stuttgart, Germany, and again at its 1912 world congress in Basel, Switzerland, the Second International had adopted resolutions insisting that should a war break out among the European imperialist powers, the duty of the working class in each country would be "to intervene in favor of its speedy termination and to do all in their power to utilize the economic and political crisis caused by the war to rouse the peoples and thereby to hasten the abolition of capitalist class rule."[1]

Instead, when the "guns of August" began blasting away, the majority of leaders of parties of the Second International in belligerent countries lined up to be counted behind the capitalists and landlords, voting for war credits in parliament and joining in patriotic calls for "defense of the fatherland." This included all but a tiny minority of the leaders of the German Social Democratic Party (SPD), the oldest and largest party in the International. The SPD had long been looked to as a model and source of fundamental Marxist education by revolutionary-minded workers throughout Europe, North America, and around the world.

HOW HAD THIS BETRAYAL of proletarian internationalist principles come to pass? What political lessons could be drawn by the revolutionary vanguard of the working class, to guard its organizations against similar degeneration and betrayals in the future? On what programmatic and strategic foundations could a new, Third, International be built?

As historical materialists, the Marxist politicians who grappled with these questions understood that the answers could not be sought merely by analyzing the incorrect ideas of the chauvinist misleaders or the pressures exerted on them by government-sponsored war hysteria. The buckling to bourgeois patriotism and the ideological rationalizations of it had to have their roots in the social conflict between classes and its reflection *inside* the organizations of the Second International. Such a capitulation was inconceivable by parties composed overwhelmingly in their *leadership,* as well as membership, of the oppressed and exploited layers that make up the vast majority of the working class.

It is this issue that Zinoviev's 1916 article addresses, concentrating on the social roots of opportunism and social patriotism in the German SPD.

At the outbreak of the war, the Bolshevik leadership in exile quickly spelled out its revolutionary alternative to the chauvinist, anti-working-class course of the majority of the Second International. Following his release from a brief period of detention by Austrian authorities, Lenin on September 6 drew up a resolution declaring that "the betrayal of socialism by most leaders of the Second International (1889–1914) signifies the ideological and political bankruptcy of the International."[2] Lenin's declaration insisted that "the defeat of the tsarist monarchy and its armies . . . would be the lesser evil by far."[3]

This "revolutionary defeatist" position stood in stark contrast to the patriotic bleatings of the capitulators in Russia and other imperialist countries. Lenin's declaration was used as the basis for a manifesto of the Bolsheviks' Central Committee published in the November 1, 1914, issue of *Sotsial-Demokrat,*[4] along with an article by Lenin urging the establishment of a Third International.

"The Second International is dead, overcome by opportunism," Lenin wrote. "Down with opportunism, and long live the Third International. . . . To the Third International falls the task of organizing the proletarian forces for a revolutionary onslaught against the capitalist governments, for civil war against the bourgeoisie of all countries for the capture of political power, for the triumph of socialism!"[5]

In other words, only a complete political *and* organizational break with the opportunists would make possible the implementation of the fundamental political perspectives adopted in 1907 and 1912 by the Second International: using "the economic and political crisis caused by the war . . . to hasten the abolition of capitalist class rule."

THESE POSITIONS WERE PRESENTED by Lenin to a February 27–March 4, 1915, conference of Bolsheviks in exile held in Switzerland. Delegates affirmed this line in a series of resolutions on the character of the war, rejection of "defense of the fatherland," and the establishment of a Third International. These documents were then circulated through the Bolsheviks' underground apparatus in Russia.[6]

Zinoviev wrote the chapter reprinted here in mid-1916, at about the same time that Lenin was completing *Imperialism: The Highest Stage of Capitalism*. Chapter 8 of that well-known book dealt briefly with the questions discussed by Zinoviev. Lenin came back to these matters in greater detail in October 1916 in an article entitled "Imperialism and the Split in Socialism." In this article Lenin summed up the political conclusions to be drawn from *Imperialism: The Highest Stage of Capitalism*, which, as he pointed out, had been "written with an eye to tsarist censorship" and thus confined largely to "exclusively theoretical, specifically economic analysis of facts."[7]

"We have to begin with as precise and full a definition of imperialism as possible," Lenin wrote in the October 1916 article. "Imperialism is a specific historical stage of capitalism." He continued:

> The supplanting of free competition by monopoly is the fundamental economic feature, the *quintessence* of imperialism. Monopoly manifests itself in five principal forms:
> (1) cartels, syndicates and trusts—the concentration of production has reached a degree which gives rise to these monopolistic associations of capitalists;
> (2) the monopolistic position of the big banks—three, four or five giant banks manipulate the whole economic life of America, France, Germany;
> (3) seizure of the sources of *raw material* by the trusts and the financial oligarchy (finance capital is monopoly industrial capital merged with bank capital);
> (4) the (economic) partition of the world by the international cartels has *begun*. There are already over *one hundred* such international cartels, which command the *entire* world market and divide it "amicably" among themselves—until war *re*divides it. The export of capital, as distinct from the export of commodities under nonmonopoly capitalism, is a highly characteristic phenomenon and is closely linked with the economic and territorial-political partition of the world;

(5) the territorial partition of the world (colonies) *is completed*.⁸

It is this historical stage of capitalism, Lenin said, that created the objective conditions in which it was possible for opportunism to develop as a consolidated political current with such widespread influence in the international workers movement. "Objectively the *opportunists* are a section of the petty bourgeoisie and of certain strata of the working class who *have been bribed* out of imperialist superprofits and converted into *watchdogs* of capitalism and *corrupters* of the labour movement."⁹

The Bolsheviks had been pointing to this connection between imperialism and opportunism in articles and resolutions over the preceding two years, Lenin said. They had concluded "that a split with the social-chauvinists was inevitable."¹⁰

LENIN POINTED OUT that key aspects of imperialism had developed in Britain while Marx and Engels were still alive, before the emergence of monopoly capitalism as a *world* system at the turn of the century. England possessed vast colonies and was reaping superprofits, due to its yet-unchallenged industrial monopoly and predominance in the world market during the mid-nineteenth century. Already at that time, Lenin continued, Marx and Engels had frequently noted the connection between these economic phenomena and the hold of class collaboration on the British labor movement. (Zinoviev cites numerous examples from Marx and Engels's writings in the article reprinted in this issue. The heart of the matter was also discussed in other writings where the term "labor aristocracy" was not itself used, such as in Engels's 1872 articles on "The Housing Question."[11]) Lenin wrote:

> Why does England's [industrial and trade] monopoly explain the (temporary) victory of opportunism in England? Because monopoly yields *superprofits,* i.e., a surplus of profits over and above the capitalist profits that are normal and customary all over the world. The capitalists *can* devote a part (and not a small one, at that!) of these superprofits to bribe *their own* workers, to create something like an alliance . . . between the workers of the given nation and their capitalists *against* the other countries.[12]

By the turn of the century, the rise of monopoly capitalism in Germany, France, Japan, and other countries had begun to challenge England's domination of industrial production and the world market, Lenin explained. (This competition narrowed the British rulers' capacity to grant concessions to substantial layers of the working class, Lenin explained in several articles written in 1912–13. By the 1890s, these changes had resulted in the unionization of broad new sections of previously unorganized workers—the so-called New Unionism; a rise in labor militancy; and mounting opposition to the traditional union officialdom's policy of political subordination to the capitalist Liberal Party.[13])

It was possible throughout much of the nineteenth century, Lenin said in "Imperialism and the Split in Socialism," "to bribe and corrupt the working class of *one* country for decades. This is now improbable, if not impossible. But on the other hand, *every* imperialist 'Great' Power can and does bribe *smaller* strata (than in England in 1848–68) of the 'labour aristocracy'.... [T]he trusts, the financial oligarchy, high prices, etc., while *enabling* the bribery of a handful in the top layers, are increasingly oppressing, crushing, ruining and torturing the *mass* of the proletariat and the semi-proletariat."[14]

Because of this, Lenin said, the policy of class collaboration with the bosses, their government, and their political parties—which during the nineteenth century had set the British labor officials apart from most other leaders in the international workers movement—had by the outbreak of World War I become the majority trend in the Second International.

Lenin's explanation that imperialism marks the triumph of monopoly capitalism as a world system makes it clear that he viewed the superprofits arising directly from colonial exploitation as only one source of the wealth that made possible the emergence of privileged labor aristocracies in the imperialist countries. Lenin, however, gave central *political* importance to colonial pillage, since attitudes on this question had become a dividing line between revolutionists and opportunists.

This analysis developed by Bolshevik leaders in the 1914–16 period was restated time and again by Lenin following the October 1917 victory in Russia. It was incorporated into the fundamental documents of the Russian Communist Party (Bolshevik) and the Communist International. A resolution adopted by the founding congress of the Comintern in March 1919, for example, explained:

> When the first shots of the imperialist carnage were fired, the leading parties of the Second

International betrayed the working class, and each, using the formula 'defence of the fatherland' as a screen, went over to the side of 'its' bourgeoisie. . . .

This was the moment of the final bankruptcy and demise of the Second International.

The general course of economic development had given the bourgeoisie in the wealthiest countries the opportunity to tempt and buy off the upper layers of the working class—the labour aristocracy—with crumbs from its enormous profits. The petty-bourgeois "camp-followers" of socialism swelled the ranks of the official social-democratic parties and gradually altered their politics in a bourgeois direction.

From the leaders of the peaceable parliamentary labour movement, the heads of the trade unions, the secretaries, editors and officials of social democracy there developed a caste—a labour bureaucracy with its own selfish group interests, essentially hostile to socialism.[15]

Note that this Comintern resolution distinguishes, as does the Zinoviev chapter, between the labor *aristocracy* and the labor *bureaucracy*. The former is a layer *of* the working class that is bought off by the bosses to act against the interests of its class as a whole. The latter—while finding its social base in and often emerging from the ranks of the labor aristocracy—is a *caste* of a petty-bourgeois character "with its own selfish group interests."

The 1919 Comintern resolution continued that, "Owing to these circumstances, the official social democracy degenerated into an anti-socialist and chauvinistic party. *Three basic currents* began to emerge within the Second International." These were:

1. The *social chauvinists,* who had "shown themselves, beyond doubt, to be the class enemies of the proletariat";

2. The *centrists,* who at the beginning of the war were "in general agreement with the social-chauvinists," then shifted toward pacifist appeals for an end to the war as mass opposition grew to the economic and human toll of the conflict, but throughout "insisted upon 'unity' with the social-chauvinists. . . . thereby preventing the workers from reaching a clear understanding of the reasons for the collapse of the Second International"; and

3. The *communist* tendency, which remained "faithful to the interests of the proletariat, proclaimed from the very start the slogan 'Turn the imperialist war into a civil war'," and "has now organized itself into the Third International."[16]

Political and theoretical antecedents

In explaining the social roots of chauvinism and class-collaborationism in the Second International, the Bolsheviks—as Zinoviev does in the accompanying article—pointed not only to the emergence of a labor aristocracy, but also to the direct influence in socialist organizations of artisans and toiling layers of the middle classes that can be political allies but are not part of the proletariat itself. This latter factor had long been pointed to by Marxists as a primary source of strength of petty-bourgeois currents such as anarchism in the workers movements of France, Spain, and Italy. In the latter half of the nineteenth century, the industrial working class in these southern European countries was still small relative to independent commodity producers and other middle layers.

"Until very recently the question of the labor aristocracy and its conservative role in the labor movement has been treated as a problem almost unique to the *British* labor movement," Zinoviev comments in the 1916 article. "The epoch of the latest form of imperialism and the events in the labor movement of the entire world in connection with the World War have posed this question on a much wider scale."

Zinoviev's assessment is correct as a generalization. Prior to the war-provoked crisis in the Second International, the Bolsheviks had not developed a full analysis of the labor aristocracy, its relationship to class-collaborationism, and its roots in imperialist superprofits.

Important additions to the theoretical and political arsenal of the working-class movement are always related to the need to come to grips *in practice* with new or unexpected developments in the class struggle. Nonetheless, there is no mechanical, one-to-one correspondence between the two. Revolutionary politicians with enough experience in the class struggle, and with knowledge of past experiences, can often discern certain features and outlines of trends before they have fully developed and exploded onto the stage of human history.

So it was with Lenin's understanding of the role of the labor aristocracy in the collapse of the Second International. That capitulation was the end-result of a long degenerative process. It was marked by changes in the social composition of the parties, by previous lapses from proletarian internationalism, by a rejection of Marxist class-struggle conceptions among growing layers of social democratic leaders, and by a drift away from the application of revolutionary strategy and tactics. The betrayal, as Lenin put it, was "no chance occurrence, sin, slip, or treachery on the part of individuals, but a social product of an entire period of history."[17]

All these portents of things to come had provoked

sharp debates in the Second International. Until 1914, however, revolutionary positions had usually won the day, at least in official resolutions. Lenin and the Bolsheviks were active participants in these political exchanges, both as they affected the Second International as a whole and its Russian adherents.

Over the course of these debates, various political strands emerged in Lenin's writings that came together in a new pattern when the outbreak of war temporarily reduced the defenders of longstanding Marxist positions to a small minority. It is useful to trace a few of these strands back to Lenin's earliest political writings—and even before.

IN THE MOST FUNDAMENTAL SENSE, the Bolsheviks' understanding of the labor aristocracy and its political role can be looked at as a special, or what in mathematics might be called a "limiting," case of the general obstacles posed to working-class consciousness and united action by the inevitable divisions inside the working class in capitalist society. These encompass both divisions among workers of different countries and within any given country.

Underlying these manifold divisions is the most basic one of all, resulting from the very condition that defines the working class as a class: the fact that workers own no land or other means of production and must sell their labor power—their capacity to work—to a capitalist in return for wages in order to feed, clothe, and house themselves and their families. Thus, competition for jobs, greater or lesser depending upon the stage of the capitalist business cycle and overall development of the economy, is a *permanent* situation for the working class, holding down wages and worsening working conditions.

Workers can counteract some of the most destructive effects of this competition by forming unions and pursuing a course of labor solidarity. Efforts along these lines are facilitated by another fundamental condition of working-class existence; that is, by the tendency under capitalism for workers to be brought together by the capitalists in giant factories, industries, and urban centers. But unionization cannot do away with this competition, as the history of the past century or the course of any strike struggle amply demonstrate.

Marx explained this phenomenon as follows in an 1866 resolution on the trade unions submitted to and adopted by the First International: "The only social power of the workmen is their number. The force of numbers, however, is broken by disunion. The disunion of the workmen is created and perpetuated by the *unavoidable competition amongst themselves.*"[18]

Aside from this unavoidable competition for jobs, and the related division between the employed and the unemployed, there is another basic *economic* source of divisions within the working class—those related to what Marx called simple and complex labor. What is involved here?

Marx explained in *Capital* that the value of a commodity is determined by "the expenditure of human labour in general" that went into producing it.[19]

The objection might be raised: But not all human labor is of the same type, is it? Some is more complex than other types, requiring greater training. Does an hour of this more complicated labor really produce only as much value as every other hour of labor?

Marx anticipated this question, explaining that by "human labour in general" he meant the expenditure of simple labour-power, i.e. of the labour-power possessed in his bodily organism by every ordinary man, on the average, without being developed in any special way.... More complex labour counts only as *intensified,* or rather *multiplied* simple labour, so that a smaller quantity of complex labour is considered equal to a larger quantity of simple labour.

Experience shows that this reduction is constantly being made. A commodity may be the outcome of the most complicated labour, but through its *value* it is posited as equal to the product of simple labour, hence it represents only a specific quantity of simple labour.[20]

Marx insisted that this "human labour in general" was not mere word play. It *"exists* in the form of average labour which, in a given society, the average person can perform, productive expenditure of a certain amount of human muscles, nerves, brain, etc," he wrote. "It is *simple* labour which any average individual can be trained to do and which in one way or another he has to perform."[21]

If complex labor counts as a multiple of simple labor, then by what social principle is the former reduced to the latter? Marx's answer in *Capital* is that "all labour of a higher, or more complicated, character than average labour is expenditure of labour-power of a more costly kind, labour-power whose production has cost more time and labour than unskilled or simple labour-power, and which therefore has a higher value."[22]

And in the chapters on economics drafted by Marx for Engels's *Anti-Dühring,* he wrote: "How then are we to solve the whole important question of the higher wages paid for compound labour? In a society of private producers, private individuals or their families pay the costs of training the skilled worker; hence the higher price paid for trained labour power also comes first of all to private individuals."[23]

In other words, the greater costs of training workers to perform complex labor is taken into account socially under capitalism through a greater value attached to the product of a given quantity of such labor. In addition, the labor power of workers performing complex labor can command a higher price—i.e., wage—on the capitalist job market. The ability of these workers to drive a harder bargain with the employers is reinforced by their greater scarcity relative to the number of workers performing simple labor, their greater likelihood of being in a hard-to-replace position in the production process, and the potential costs to the boss of training a replacement.

This, then, is the way the relationship of simple and complex labor works out—in theory.

But what about in the real world?

For purposes of simplification, Marx in *Capital* presented a model of a "pure" capitalist society, divided by and large between two categories of individuals: a tiny handful of capitalists who own all the means of production, and the mass of workers who have only their labor power to sell and are equal to each other in all respects. Of course, no such capitalist society exists, ever did, or ever could. Not only are there all sorts of intermediate layers of small farmers, other independent commodity producers, shopkeepers, professionals, and so on, but the working class itself is differentiated and stratified in countless ways.

In the initial period of capitalism's development, specialized crafts performing complex labor still played a major, sometimes predominant, role in manufacturing. Marx pointed out that the historical progress of industrial capitalism—with its interchangeable parts, mass-production techniques, and mechanization—greatly increased the role of simple, average labor in capitalist production and tended to homogenize job categories in this regard.

In modern capitalism, Marx wrote, "Not only the category, labour, but labour in reality has here become the means of creating wealth in general, and has ceased to be organically linked with particular individuals in any specific form. Such a state of affairs is at its most developed in the most modern form of existence of bourgeois society—in the United States. Here, then, for the first time, the . . . abstraction of the category 'labour', 'labour as such', labour pure and simple, becomes true in practice."[24]

Thus, Marx explained in *Capital,* "in place of the hierarchy of specialized workers that characterizes [early capitalist] manufacture, there appears, in the automatic factory, a tendency to equalize and reduce to an identical level every kind of work that has to be done by the minders of the machines; in place of the artificially produced distinctions between the specialized workers, it is natural differences of age and sex that predominate."[25]

THIS LAST OBSERVATION by Marx points to the most important consideration, because in real as opposed to "pure" capitalist society these "extraeconomic" divisions actually play the predominant role in determining differentiations in wages and conditions on and off the job. These divisions can be based on physical differences (age, race, or sex), sheer prejudice (national origin), or social power (union vs. nonunion). All are made use of by the employers to pit worker against worker.

Marx took note of this reality in an important and concise explanation in *Capital*. "The distinction between higher and simple labour, 'skilled labour' and 'unskilled labor'," he wrote, "rests in part on pure illusion or, to say the least, on distinctions that have long since ceased to be real, and survive only by virtue of a traditional convention; and in part on the helpless condition of some sections of the working class, a condition that prevents them from exacting equally with the rest the value of their labour-power."[26]

The part of Marx's explanation *before* the semicolon refers to what we in the United States today call "job trusts." Certain groups of workers—by dint of exclusive craft-union structures that effectively keep out Blacks and women, and strictly limit new entrants in general—have been able to maintain relatively high wage levels. These greater benefits derive not from the current complexity of their labor, but, in Marx's words, from considerations that have "long since ceased to be real, and survive only by virtue of a traditional convention." A convention enforced by the job trust. This occurs *in spite of* the homogenization of labor with the progress of mechanization.

The part of Marx's explanation *after* the semicolon, on the other hand, points to stratifications in the working class that also have no direct economic source, but instead result from social *discrimination*. The "helpless condition" referred to by Marx can be attributable to many kinds of discrimination—for reasons of age, sex, race, country of origin, physical handicap, or whatever. Despite the high level of skill and experience involved in the labor performed by sewing-machine operators in the U.S. garment industry today, for example, the fact that most of them are women and immigrants prevents them "from exacting equally with the rest the value of their labour power"; they are among the lowest-paid workers in the United States, with some of the worst job conditions.

In *Capital,* Marx dealt at some length with how British capitalists in the nineteenth century took advantage of the prevailing social attitudes toward women and children to superexploit them and to deprive them of the value of their labor power on a par with adult male workers, that is, to deny them equal pay for equal work. The result was a drastic lowering of the wages and degradation of the conditions of the entire working class, male and female, adult and child. Three years after the publication of the first volume of *Capital,* in an April 1870 letter to two supporters of the First International in the United States, Marx explained another case in point, this time the use of prejudice based on national oppression. Marx wrote:

> Every industrial and commercial centre in England now possesses a working class divided into two *hostile* camps, English proletarians and Irish proletarians. The ordinary English worker hates the Irish worker as a competitor who lowers his standard of life. In relation to the Irish worker he regards himself as a member of the *ruling* nation and consequently he becomes a tool of the English aristocrats and capitalists *against Ireland,* thus strengthening their domination *over himself.* He cherishes religious, social, and national prejudices against the Irish worker. His attitude towards him is much the same as that of the "poor whites" to the Negroes in the former slave states of the U.S.A. The Irishman pays him back with interest in his

own money. He sees in the English worker both the accomplice and the stupid tool of the *English rulers in Ireland.*

This antagonism is artificially kept alive and intensified by the press, the pulpit, the comic papers, in short, by all the means at the disposal of the ruling classes. *This antagonism* is the *secret of the impotence of the English working class,* despite its organization. It is the secret by which the capitalist class maintains its power. And the latter is quite aware of this.[27]

THIS 1870 LETTER calls attention to a political issue of growing importance today—the connection between struggles by oppressed nationalities and immigrant workers in the imperialist countries, and anti-imperialist struggles by the workers and peasants of Asia, Africa, and Latin America. Marx's message for English workers in the above-cited letter is applicable today to the labor movement in all the imperialist countries with regard to solidarity with national liberation struggles: "The *national emancipation of Ireland* is not a question of abstract justice or humanitarian sentiment but *the first condition of their own social emancipation.*"[28]

Engels, too, addressed this question of the employers' use of national divisions in the working class. In an 1892 letter to a workers' leader in the United States, Engels pointed out some obstacles to winning English-speaking U.S. workers to a class-struggle perspective. He explained:

> Your great obstacle in America, it seems to me, lies in the exceptional position of the native

workers. Up to 1848 one could only speak of the permanent native working class as an exception: the small beginnings of it in the cities in the East could always hope to become farmers or bourgeois. Now a native working class has developed and is also to a large extent organized in trade unions. But it still assumes an aristocratic posture and wherever possible leaves the ordinary badly paid occupations to the immigrants, of whom only a small section enter the aristocratic trades. These immigrants, however, are divided into different nationalities and understand neither one another nor, for the most part, the language of the country [English]. And your bourgeoisie knows much better even than the Austrian Government how to play off one nationality against the other: Jews, Italians, Bohemians, etc., against Germans and Irish, and each one against the other, so that differences in the living standards of the workers exist, I believe, in New York to an extent unheard-of elsewhere.

And added to this is the total indifference of a society which has grown up on a purely capitalist basis . . . towards the human beings who succumb in the competitive struggle: "there will be plenty more, and more than we want, of these damned Dutchmen, Irishmen, Italians, Jews and Hungarians"; and, to cap it all, John Chinaman stands in the background, who far surpasses them all in his ability to live on next to nothing.[29]

Twenty-six years later, in *Imperialism: The Highest Stage of Capitalism,* Lenin pointed out that these divisions in the U.S. working class remained basically unchanged: "In the United States, immigrants from Eastern and Southern Europe are engaged in the most poorly paid jobs, while American workers provide the highest percentage of overseers or of the better-paid workers. Imperialism has the tendency to create privileged sections also among the workers, and to detach them from the broad masses of the proletariat."[30]

And three years later, in 1919, Lenin again stressed that the imperialist bourgeoisies "shift the burden of the worst paid and hardest work to backward workers brought into the country, and enhance the privileges of the 'labour aristocracy' as compared with the majority of the working class."[31]

IN AN EFFORT TO COMBAT the pernicious effects of competition and division on their living standards and job conditions, workers since the industrial revolution in the last half of the eighteenth century have banded together in collective struggle, forming trade unions. At first, these tended to be organized along lines of crafts or skills. As a rule, only the most skilled layers of the working class were organized, leaving the big majority of unskilled workers in the large factories without any union protection.

Later, unions structured along industrial lines began to be organized and to win battles for recognition from the bosses. This occurred around the turn of the century in some European countries, but not until the 1930s in the United States. While these unions were open to all workers in a given factory or industry, in most countries the organized labor movement still encompassed only a minority of the working class; in the United States the figure has never risen much above one-third, and today is below one-quarter. Workers not organized by the unions must endure the worst blows from economic competition and social discrimination, generally receiving much lower wages and working under the most intensive and unsafe conditions.

Unions not only mark an important step forward for the working class, but are an inevitable product of its class struggle against the unceasing drive by the bosses to maximize profits at workers' expense. They are the most massive and powerful institutions of the working class.

Marxists have always understood, however, that these mighty economic organizations alone are insufficient to advance the interests of the working class as a whole, and therefore in the long run are also insufficient to safeguard the interests of any particular section of the working class. Marx's 1866 resolution on trade unions drafted for the First International offered the following explanation:

> Trades' Unions originally sprang up from the *spontaneous* attempts of workmen at removing or at least checking that competition [among them], in order to conquer such terms of contract as might raise them at least above the condition of mere slaves. The immediate object of Trades' Unions was therefore confined to everyday necessities, to expediencies for the obstruction of the incessant encroachments of capital, in one word, to questions of wages and time of labour.
>
> This activity of the Trades' Unions is not only legitimate, it is necessary. It cannot be dispensed with so long as the present system of production lasts. On the contrary, it must be generalised by the formation and the combination of Trades' Unions throughout all countries.

Having established the origins and necessity of unions, the 1866 resolution continued:

> Too exclusively bent upon the local and immediate struggles with capital, the Trades' Unions have not yet fully understood their power of acting against the system of wage slavery itself. They therefore kept too much aloof from general social and political movements. . . .
> Apart from their original purposes, they must now learn to act deliberately as organizing centres of the working class in the broad interest of its *complete emancipation*. They must aid every social and political movement tending in that direction. Considering themselves and acting as the champions and representatives of the whole working class, they cannot fail to enlist the nonsociety [unorganized or nonunion] men into their ranks. They must look carefully after the interests of the worst paid trades, such as the agricultural labourers, rendered powerless by exceptional circumstances. They must convince the world at large that their efforts, far from being narrow and selfish, aim at the emancipation of the downtrodden millions.[32]

This revolutionary strategy for the trade unions brings us back more directly to the strands in Lenin's early political writings that were subsequently woven together into the Bolsheviks' understanding of the social roots of class-collaborationism. The political orientation contained in Marx's 1866 resolution, as well as in the concluding portion of his pamphlet *Wages, Price, and Profit* written the previous year,[33] were at the heart of Lenin's program for the tasks of the Russian proletariat and its vanguard party at the turn of the century, when the Russian Social Democratic Labor Party was founded.

As early as 1894, well before the formation of the RSDLP, Lenin had stressed in a major programmatic article that underlying all the activities of proletarian revolutionists in Russia "is the common conviction that the Russian worker is the sole and natural representative of Russia's entire working and exploited population." Lenin continued:

> The worker cannot fail to see that he is oppressed by *capital*, that his struggle has to be waged against the bourgeois *class*. And this struggle, aimed at satisfying his immediate economic needs, at improving his material conditions, inevitably demands that the workers organise, and inevitably becomes a war not against individuals, but against a *class*, the class which oppresses and crushes the working people not only in the factories, but everywhere.
>
> That is why the factory worker is none other than the foremost representative of the entire exploited population. And in order that he may fulfil his function of representative in an organised, sustained struggle . . . all that is needed is simply *to make him understand his position*, to make him understand the political and economic structure of the system that oppresses him, and the necessity and inevitability of class antagonisms under this system.
>
> This position of the factory worker in the general system of capitalist relations makes him the sole fighter for the emancipation of the working

class, for only the higher stage of development of capitalism, large-scale machine industry, creates the material conditions and the social forces necessary for this struggle.[34]

One of Lenin's earliest political battles inside the RSDLP was against the so-called Economist current, which sought to limit social democratic activity to trade union-type matters in the factories and to solely those political questions directly related to economic conditions of the workers. Lenin answered these anti-Marxist ideas in his well-known 1902 pamphlet, *What Is To Be Done?* Lenin wrote:

> Social-Democracy leads the struggle of the working class, not only for better terms for the sale of labour-power, but for the abolition of the social system that compels the propertyless to sell themselves to the rich. Social-Democracy represents the working class, not in its relation to a given group of employers alone, but in its relation to all classes of modern society and to the state as an organised political force.[35]

Responding to the Economists' extremely narrow conception of working-class political action, Lenin continued:

> *Any and every* manifestation of police tyranny and autocratic outrage, not only in connection with the economic struggle, is not one whit less "widely applicable" as a means of "drawing in" the masses.[36]

And further on in the pamphlet:

> Working-class consciousness cannot be genuine political consciousness unless the workers are trained to respond to *all* cases of tyranny, oppression, violence, and abuse, no matter *what class* is affected—unless they are trained, moreover, to respond from a Social-Democratic point of view and no other.[37] [The term "Social Democrat" was used both by the revolutionary and reformist wings of the Second International; following the October 1917 revolution in Russia, both the Bolshevik Party and the new International founded two years later rejected the continued use of the term and readopted the name "Communist," used by Marx and Engels in the 1848 *Manifesto of the Communist Party*.—S.C.]

If revolutionists carry out their political work in the factories in this spirit, Lenin said, then:

> The most backward worker will understand, *or will feel,* that the students and religious sects, the peasants and the authors are being abused and outraged by those same dark forces that are oppressing and crushing him at every step of his life. Feeling that, he will himself be filled with an irresistible desire to react, and he will know how to hoot the censors one day, on another day to demonstrate outside the house of a governor who has brutally suppressed a peasant uprising, on still another day to teach a lesson to the gendarmes in surplices who are doing the work of the Holy Inquisition, etc.[38]

Summarizing the Marxist political viewpoint, Lenin explained:

Class political consciousness can be brought to the workers *only from without*, that is, only from outside the economic struggle, from outside the sphere of relations between workers and employers. The sphere from which alone it is possible to obtain this knowledge is the sphere of relationships of *all* classes. . . .

The Social Democrat's ideal should not be the trade-union secretary, but *the tribune of the people,* who is able to react to every manifestation of tyranny and oppression, no matter where it appears, no matter what stratum or class of the people it affects; who is able to generalise all these manifestations and produce a single picture of police violence and capitalist exploitation; who is able to take advantage of every event, however small, in order to set forth *before all* his socialist convictions and his democratic demands, in order to clarify for *all* and everyone the world-historic significance of the struggle for the emancipation of the proletariat.[39]

It is not enough to agree that the working class needs to be drawn into politics, Lenin stressed. The capitalist rulers can easily live with the kind of narrow political involvement advocated by the Economists, which remained in the framework of the private property system and capitalist social relations. "Trade-unionist politics of the working class," Lenin said, "is precisely *bourgeois politics* of the working class."[40]

In his writings from this period, Lenin cited examples of some of the worst fruits of such a narrow, craft approach in the world labor movement. He pointed to the so-called "Birmingham Alliances" in the 1890s, whereby trade union officials in that British city collaborated with the bosses to try to maintain high prices for metal products, at the expense of the working class and population as a whole. (This is mindful of the alliance today between many U.S. labor officials and big business to demand import barriers that raise prices on goods sold in this country.)

During a speech at the August 1903 Second Congress of the RSDLP, Lenin pointed to another example—a group of British coal miners in the 1880s who extracted a seven-hour day from the coal bosses for a skilled layer of workers, in exchange for opposing labor's efforts to secure legislation for an eight-hour day for the entire British working class.

During the first decade of this century, Lenin also joined in the debates in the Second International against the revisionist current, associated most prominently with German SPD leader Eduard Bernstein. The revisionists rejected Marx and Engels's fundamental economic and political conclusions and replaced the Marxist class-struggle program and strategy with a class-collaborationist approach based on the utopian idea of a peaceful evolution of capitalism into socialism. The unions and workers parties were to operate as pressure groups on the state—now claimed to be a neutral institution, standing above the class struggle and able to reflect and arbitrate conflicting class interests. In this way, the labor movement could promote a gradual transition by means of social democratic electoral victories and the steady accumulation of economic and political reform measures in the legislature.

Some of Lenin's polemical writings on these questions

contain little or nothing of his subsequent emphasis on the role of a labor aristocracy and imperialist superprofits in fostering opportunism in the Second International. This is true, for example, of his 1908 article "Marxism and Revisionism" and his 1910 article "Differences in the European Labour Movement."

Both articles recognized that these revisionist views must have a social cause. "The inevitability of revisionism is determined by its class roots in modern society," Lenin wrote in 1908.[41] And in 1910, "There must be deep-rooted causes in the economic system and in the character of the development of all capitalist countries which constantly give rise to these departures."[42]

In both articles, however, Lenin's explanation was limited to only *one* of the two sources explored in the accompanying 1916 Zinoviev article and in later Bolshevik writings—i.e., to the direct influence of petty-bourgeois and petty-bourgeoisified layers in the party. In the 1910 article, Lenin wrote: "There is not and cannot be a Chinese wall between the proletariat and the sections of the petty bourgeoisie in contact with it, including the peasantry. It is clear that the passing of certain individuals, groups and sections of the petty bourgeoisie into the ranks of the proletariat is bound, in its turn, to give rise to vacillations in the tactics of the latter."[43]

Nevertheless, in an article written even earlier than either of these, Lenin *did* comment at some length on matters that anticipate quite closely his post-1914 writings on the social roots of opportunism. This is his account of the 1907 world congress of the Second International held in Stuttgart. The debates at that congress around a range of political questions are rich in lessons for revolutionary-minded workers, but Lenin's comments on two contested issues in particular are most relevant to the matters at hand in this article.

First, a debate took place around an effort, led by the majority of the German SPD delegation, to reverse the Second International's previous steadfast opposition to colonialism. The gathering's colonial commission inserted a sentence into its proposed resolution explaining that socialists were not opposed in principle to all colonialism, since under a socialist government such policies could allegedly play a "civilizing" role. Among the most recalcitrant proponents of this position, which was defeated by the congress, were those SPD delegates representing the German trade union officialdom.

Commenting on the outcome of this debate, Lenin wrote: "The combined vote of the small nations, which either do not pursue a colonial policy, or which suffer from it, outweighed the vote of nations where even the proletariat has been somewhat infected with the lust of conquest." Expanding on this point, Lenin continued:

> This vote on the colonial question is of very great importance. First, it strikingly showed up socialist opportunism, which succumbs to bourgeois blandishments. Secondly, it revealed a negative feature in the European labour movement, one that can do no little harm to the proletarian cause, and for that reason should receive serious attention. . . .
>
> The non-propertied, but non-working, class is incapable of overthrowing the exploiters. Only the proletarian class, which maintains the whole of society, can bring about the social revolution. However, as a result of the extensive colonial policy, the European proletarian *partly* finds himself in a position when it is *not* his labour, but the labour of

the practically enslaved natives in the colonies, that maintains the whole of society. . . .

In certain countries this provides the material and economic basis for infecting the proletariat with colonial chauvinism. Of course, this may be only a temporary phenomenon, but the evil must nonetheless be clearly realised and its causes understood in order to be able to rally the proletariat of all countries for the struggle against such opportunism. This struggle is bound to be victorious, since the "privileged" nations are a diminishing fraction of the capitalist nations.[44]

The other relevant debate at Stuttgart was around the question of socialist policy toward immigration and foreign-born workers.

THE U.S. SOCIALIST PARTY, along with the officialdom of the American Federation of Labor (AFL) (which was not affiliated with the SP or the Second International), held the chauvinist position of calling on the capitalist government to slam shut the door on immigrant workers, especially those from China and other Asian nations. Some SP leaders, such as Victor Berger of Milwaukee, openly proclaimed the inferiority of Asian and Black peoples and warned of the "yellow peril" to white womanhood and to the "purity" of the white race. The centrist majority conciliated with these views, keeping the most overtly racist language out of resolutions, but maintaining the general line nonetheless.

A left-wing minority of SP leaders strongly condemned the party's position. Eugene V. Debs called it "utterly unsocialistic, reactionary, and in truth outrageous."[45]

The big majority of the SP delegation came to Stuttgart in 1907 hoping that the growing weight of revisionist currents in the Second International might enable it to get the blessings of the congress for its anti-internationalist policy. This attempt did not succeed.

Commenting on what he called the "narrow, craft interests" underlying the SP's proposal, Lenin noted: "This is the same spirit of aristocratism that one finds among workers in some of the 'civilised' countries, who derive certain advantages from their privileged position, and are, therefore, inclined to forget the need for international class solidarity."[46]

In 1907, however, the political influence of the opportunist currents was still not predominant in the Second International. "On the whole," Lenin concluded, "the Stuttgart Congress brought into sharp contrast the opportunist and revolutionary wings of the international Social-Democratic movement on a number of cardinal issues and decided these issues in the spirit of revolutionary Marxism."[47]

A series of articles by Lenin in 1912–13 on rising union militancy and pressures for independent labor political action in Britain came back to some of the above themes as they applied to that country in particular.

And in an article from June 1914, two months before the outbreak of world war, Lenin said the following about a study of circulation figures inside Russia of the press of the Bolshevik and opportunist Menshevik wings of the RSDLP: "Our conjecture is that the liquidators [Mensheviks] unite the minority of the higher-paid workers in certain sections of industry. It has been observed all over the world that such workers cling to liberal and opportunist ideas." The article referred to this minority of workers as "the labour aristocracy."[48]

Labor aristocracy and labor bureaucracy

As Zinoviev explains, however, these various strands in Lenin's writings were put together as a coherent whole by the Bolsheviks only under the impact of World War I and the pressing political necessity to explain the causes of the collapse of the Second International. This analysis—explored in depth by Zinoviev in 1916 with reference to the particular case of Germany—was perhaps generalized most concisely in the 1915 article jointly written by Lenin and Zinoviev, entitled, "Socialism and War: The Attitude of the R.S.D.L.P. Towards the War."

Opportunism and social patriotism, they wrote, are the product of "an alliance of a section of the radical petty bourgeoisie and a tiny section of privileged workers, with their 'own' national bourgeoisie, against the mass of the proletariat."[49]

This precise phrase, or slight variations of it, appears time and again throughout Lenin's writings and Bolshevik and Comintern documents over the subsequent seven or eight years. Moreover, the two social layers cited by it are exactly those analyzed by Zinoviev in the 1916 article as the social base of the opportunist labor bureaucracy in Germany: 1) what he calls the "petty-bourgeois camp-followers" of the German SPD; and 2) the labor aristocracy.

Zinoviev and Lenin were careful in their joint article "Socialism and War" to stress that the policies of the social patriots run directly counter to the interests of the vast majority of workers in the imperialist countries. They wrote:

> Opportunism and social-chauvinism stand on a common economic basis—the interests of a

thin crust of privileged workers and of the petty bourgeoisie, who are defending their privileged position, their "right" to some modicum of the profits that their "own" national bourgeoisie obtain from robbing other nations, from the advantages of their Great-Power status, etc.

Opportunism and social-chauvinism have the same politico-ideological content—class collaboration instead of the class struggle, renunciation of revolutionary methods of struggle, helping one's "own" government in its embarrassed situation, instead of taking advantage of these embarrassments so as to advance the revolution.[50]

The assessment that the class-collaborationist and national-chauvinist policies of the labor officialdom have their social basis only in a more or less narrow layer of privileged workers is true despite the fact that, relative to the toilers in the oppressed nations, *wide layers* of workers in the imperialist countries enjoy much higher living standards. It is also true despite the fact that the greater overall social wealth and prosperity in the imperialist countries, made possible in part by pillage of the colonial peoples, has undoubtedly served to buffer the sharpness of the class struggle in these countries and to hold back the eruption of revolutionary crises threatening capitalist rule.

Many factors other than monopoly superprofits per se come into play in both these regards.

The higher living standards in the industrially advanced countries are a combined product of big historic advances in agricultural and industrial productivity and of hard-fought class battles by labor and the oppressed to raise the level of their wages and their conditions at home and on the job. Under these circumstances, imperialist superprofits—especially during periods of rapid economic expansion—can significantly widen the capitalists' latitude to grant concessions in order to promote social peace, either at the factory and industry level or through broader social welfare policies. But workers get nothing that they haven't labored and fought for.

Despite imperialist superprofits throughout the twentieth century, moreover, the working class in the imperialist countries has time and again demonstrated its potential to act as a leading force for progressive and even revolutionary social change. There have been revolutionary and prerevolutionary situations in Europe at the close of World War I, in the years just before and just after World War II, and on a lesser scale in parts of southern Europe in the late 1960s and first half of the 1970s, particularly in Portugal.

In all these cases, the class-collaborationist policies of the Social Democratic and Stalinist labor misleaders bore central responsibility for the eventual defeat of promising opportunities for the workers and farmers to take power from the hands of the capitalist ruling classes.

While there have been no revolutionary or prerevolutionary situations in North America, a mass labor radicalization in the 1930s succeeded in unionizing most basic industry, posed the need for independent working-class political action (in Canada actually leading to the consolidation at the end of World War II of a union-based labor party), and helped lay the foundation for the mass civil rights struggles that toppled Jim Crow segregation in the 1950s and 1960s.

The opportunist and chauvinist policies of the labor bureaucracy actually run counter not only to the historical class *political* interests of even the most privileged layers of workers in abolishing capitalist exploitation once and for all, but even operate against all but their most temporary and short-run *economic* interests, as well. Whatever crumbs they may gain from imperialist profits in the form of concessions from the bosses, these workers come nowhere near receiving back in wages the value produced by their labor and expropriated from them as profits by the bosses. They remain exploited, along with the rest of their class.

WHAT'S MORE, while tossing crumbs from their superprofits to a thin layer of workers, the bosses themselves keep the whole cookie, so to speak, thereby increasing their relative wealth and their social and economic power over the entire working class year by year. This steadily alters the relationship of class forces on the economic level to the advantage of the bosses. It gives them a stronger bargaining position at contract time, and allows them to hold out longer against strike struggles. By supplanting "we," the workers and oppressed, with "we," the workers and employers, the power of the unions is gradually eroded. The bosses find it easier to roll back wages and work rules. New technology, rather than reducing workers' hours and easing their labors, leads to layoffs, speedup, and overtime.

This has, in fact, been the trend in imperialist countries since the epoch of imperialism opened at the beginning of this century, despite substantial concessions by the capitalists stemming from their colonial superprofits. Nowhere has the working class or any section of it been able to accumulate sufficient wealth to transform itself from a class of wage-earners into a class of property-holders. More than a century of experience has confirmed Marx's conclusion that only a socialist revolution aimed at the eventual abolition of the wage system can emancipate the working class from exploitation.

The toilers' only weapon against the growing power of the capitalists is their independent economic and political organization to pursue a consistent class-struggle course against the rulers. The end result of such a revolutionary course is the conquest of political power and the establishment of a workers and farmers government that can lead the workers to expropriate the capitalists and begin the construction of socialism.

Those privileged layers of the working class in imperialist countries who are cajoled by concessions from the capitalists into believing that they benefit from the foreign policy of the ruling class have simply fallen for the false idea perpetuated by schools, press, and pulpit that workers and bosses have at least some common interests. Marx refuted this illusion in a series of articles published for the education of German workers in 1849 that are collected in the pamphlet *Wage Labour and Capital*.

"*The interests of capital and the interests of wage labour are diametrically opposed,*" Marx insisted. This is true of even the best conditions under capitalism, when workers' real wages are increasing, Marx explained. He developed this point in the following manner:

> If, for instance, in times when business is good, wages rise by five per cent, profit on the other hand by thirty per cent, then the comparative, the relative wages, have not *increased* but *decreased*.
>
> Thus if the income of the worker increases

with the rapid growth of capital [such as is made possible by imperialist pillage, we can add for the purposes of this article—S.C.], the social gulf that separates the worker from the capitalist increases at the same time, and the power of capital over labour, the dependence of labour on capital, likewise increases at the same time.

To say that the worker has an interest in the rapid growth of capital [or imperialist capital—S.C.] is only to say that the more rapidly the worker increases the wealth of others, the richer will be the crumbs that fall to him, the greater is the number of workers that can be employed and called into existence, the more can the mass of slaves dependent on capital be increased. . . . The material position of the workers has improved, but at the cost of his social position. The social gulf that divides him from the capitalist has widened.[51]

Contrary to the bosses' claims, wages do not come out of a pie of rigidly fixed size, with workers condemned merely to fight among themselves for the biggest slice. The size of the wages pie itself is determined by the class struggle.

In periods of economic expansion, unemployment goes down, weakening one of the major clubs used by employers against workers to keep them disciplined. If workers are unionized, they can win wage increases and better working conditions during such periods. Over time, this can result in an increase in what Marx called the historical and moral element in the determination of wages; in plain words, the working class has won higher living standards.

In periods of capitalist economic stagnation, such as

over the past decade, overall unemployment levels rise, and workers bargain from a weakened position. This is all the more true if their unions have been debilitated as a result of class-collaborationist policies during the previous period of prosperity. The wages workers lose during such a period wind up not in the pockets of other workers, either at home or abroad, but in the bosses' coffers.

THERE IS A SECOND SENSE in which the labor aristocracy's belief that it has a stake in imperialism is based on false consciousness promoted by the bosses and labor bureaucrats. Like other divisions in the working class perpetuated by the employers, whether based on race, sex, or whatever, the end result of the gulf between the labor aristocracy and the rest of the class is to keep the mass of workers in jobs with low wages and poor working conditions. This, in turn, heightens competition and drags down the wages and job conditions of the working class as a whole, including its top layers. The capitalists try to exploit and deepen these divisions during periods when they are intensifying austerity, aiming to pit workers against each other and break their unity against the employers.

Only labor solidarity strengthens the hand of the working class to the greatest extent possible in its tug of war with the employers over the division of the wealth produced by the labor of the workers. This extends all the way from solidarity with workers abroad, to support for affirmative action for women and oppressed minorities, to solidarity on the job and between unions during strikes.

Zinoviev referred to these points, too, in his 1916 article:

To foster splits between the various strata of the working class, to promote competition among them, to segregate the upper stratum from the rest by corrupting it and by making it an agency for bourgeois "respectability"—that is entirely in the interests of the bourgeoisie. Even if we were to disregard the *political* interests of the working class, the social chauvinists would still be traitors to the cause of the workers. For even in the field of protecting the *economic* interests they cannot see further than their noses. They identify economic interests with a temporary advantage amounting to a few more pennies. They split the working class inside of every country and thereby intensify and aggravate the split between the working classes of the various countries.

The union bureaucracy, however, *is* directly paid off by the capitalist class. These officials produce nothing of value, either in the scientific or the everyday use of the term. In addition to what they skim from workers' union dues, the bureaucrats receive all sorts of gifts, "perks," positions on "Blue Ribbon" commissions, and additional sources of income in return for services rendered.

These bureaucrats, of course, do not and could not maintain their stranglehold over the unions merely by relying on rigged elections and threats of thuggery. They need a social base in the labor movement that can help them promote their class-collaborationist perspectives and perpetuate their control. The officialdom finds this base among the labor aristocracy. The higher living standards and greater security enjoyed by these workers make them particularly susceptible to the idea, promoted by the bosses and bureaucrats, that they live well because "their" company is doing well. This is used to convince these workers that they have a greater stake in "national" rather than class interests; that they benefit from discrimination against oppressed nationalities and women; that immigrants are a threat to them; and that capitalism deserves their support. In other words, what's good for General Motors is good for the USA—and good for me!

To the extent that workers hold these views, even those in the labor aristocracy, they are victims of *false* consciousness. In accepting these ideas, they are led to act against their own class interests as workers.

Political and strategic conclusions

What concrete political, strategic, and tactical conclusions did Lenin and the Bolsheviks draw with the help of their analysis of the social roots of opportunism?

First, they fought inside the world workers movement for recognition that the majority of the officialdom of the Second International had deserted the working class and gone over to the enemy class, the imperialists. There could be no political or organizational reconciliation with these misleaders, who constituted a petty-bourgeois social caste with class interests opposed to those of the workers. The Second International was dead; the communist tendency had to launch a new, Third International to replace it.

Revolutionary workers had to turn their backs once and for all on the opportunist labor bureaucracy, and on the centrist misleaders who sought to make excuses for the opportunists and patch the bankrupt International back together. Did this mean, however, that communists should turn their backs on the hundreds of thousands of workers in parties and unions who still were confused and looked to these officials as their leaders?

No. In fact, it did not even mean that communists should write off winning supporters from the ranks of the labor aristocracy, which—unlike the bureaucracy—was composed of *workers* whose actual class interests lay with those of the rest of their class, not with the bosses and the bosses' government. Sections of highly skilled and well-paid workers could initiate significant labor struggles, adopt advanced political and social positions, and provide needed solidarity with struggles of other working people at home and abroad. The Bolsheviks did not dismiss potential support from these quarters.

"Neither we nor anyone else can calculate precisely what portion of the proletariat is following and will follow the social-chauvinists and opportunists," Lenin wrote in his 1916 article "Imperialism and the Split in Socialism." "This will be revealed only by the struggle, it will be definitely decided only by the socialist revolution."[52]

AT THE SAME TIME, Lenin and the Bolsheviks did not allow this stance toward even the most privileged wage workers to blind them to the general *trends* that had been revealed by history and that had to be the bedrock of communist strategy and tactics. Lenin wrote in "Imperialism and the Split in Socialism":

> We know for certain that the "defenders of the fatherland" in the imperialist war *represent* only a minority. And it is therefore our duty, if we wish to remain socialists, to go down *lower* and *deeper* to the real masses; this is the whole meaning and the whole purport of the struggle against opportunism.
>
> By exposing the fact that the opportunists

and social-chauvinists are in reality betraying
and selling [out] the interests of the masses, that
they are defending the temporary privileges
of a minority of the workers, that they are the
vehicles of bourgeois ideas and influences, that
they are really allies and agents of the bourgeoisie,
we teach the masses to appreciate their true
political interests, to fight for socialism and for
the revolution through all the long and painful
vicissitudes of imperialist wars and imperialist
armistices.

"This," Lenin said, "is the essence of Marxist tactics."[53]

Did this imply that communists should turn their backs on the existing trade unions, which more often than not organized only a minority of the working class, frequently the more skilled and highly paid layers?

To the contrary. The false charge that Lenin's political strategy led to this practical conclusion had already been leveled against him by the Economists back in 1903, based on snippets from *What Is to Be Done?* ripped out of context. Lenin answered this accusation in a speech to the RSDLP's second congress that year. He asked:

Have I not said time and again that the shortage
of fully class-conscious workers, worker-leaders,
and worker-revolutionaries is, in fact, the greatest
deficiency in our movement? Have I not said that
the training of such worker-revolutionaries must be
our immediate task? Is there no mention [in *What
Is To Be Done?*] of the importance of developing
a trade-union movement and creating a special
trade-union literature? Is not a desperate struggle
waged there against every attempt to lower the level

of the advanced workers to that of the masses, or of the average workers?[54]

During the first five years of the Communist International, the Bolshevik leadership simultaneously placed their view of the labor aristocracy right at the heart of major programmatic documents and fought a vigorous battle to orient communists to active participation in the trade unions. They saw this as a central axis of the fight *against* the policies of the opportunist bureaucracy, backed by layers of privileged workers.

L<small>ENIN AND OTHER LEADERS</small> polemicized time and again against those ultraleft currents in the Comintern who had drawn the fallacious conclusion from the bankruptcy of the labor officialdom that revolutionists must withdraw from the existing trade unions, advocate their destruction, and attempt to set up "revolutionary" unions to rival these established structures.

Writing shortly before the 1920 second Comintern congress, in his pamphlet *"Left-Wing" Communism: An Infantile Disorder,* Lenin sought to lift the question out of the narrow framework of the leftists and place it in a broader historical context:

> The trade unions were a tremendous step forward for the working class in the early days of capitalist development, inasmuch as they marked a transition from the workers' disunity and helplessness to the *rudiments* of class organisation. When the *revolutionary party of the proletariat,* the *highest* form of proletarian class organisation, began to take shape . . . the trade unions inevitably

began to reveal *certain* reactionary features, a certain craft narrow-mindedness, a certain tendency to be non-political, a certain inertness, etc. However, the development of the proletariat did not, and could not, proceed anywhere in the world otherwise than through the trade unions, through reciprocal action between them and the party of the working class.[55]

Lenin continued:

> We are waging a struggle against the "labour aristocracy" in the name of the masses of the workers and in order to win them over to our side; we are waging the struggle against the opportunist and social-chauvinist leaders in order to win the working class over to our side. It would be absurd to forget this most elementary and most self-evident truth. Yet it is this very absurdity that the German "Left" Communists perpetrate when, *because* of the reactionary and counterrevolutionary character of the trade union *top leadership*, they jump to the conclusion . . . we must withdraw from the trade unions, refuse to work in them, and create new and *artificial* forms of labour organisation.
>
> This is so unpardonable a blunder that it is tantamount to the greatest service Communists could render the bourgeoisie. . . . To refuse to work in the reactionary trade unions means leaving the insufficiently developed or backward masses of workers under the influence of the reactionary leaders, the agents of the bourgeoisie, the labour aristocrats.[56]

Lenin's views were debated and affirmed in resolutions adopted by the second Comintern congress in 1920, and again by the third congress in 1921, which declared: "The principal task of all Communists over the next period, is to wage a firm and victorious struggle to win the majority of the workers organized in the trade unions. The Communist must not be discouraged by the present reactionary mood of the labour unions, but must try to overcome all resistance and by actively participating in their day-to-day struggle, win the unions to Communism. The true measure of the strength of a Communist Party is the influence it has on the mass of trade unionists."[57]

A GOOD EXAMPLE of a concrete application of this general Comintern policy was its attitude toward participation by communist workers in the American Federation of Labor in the United States. With the significant exception of the United Mine Workers, AFL unions were organized almost exclusively along craft lines. The federation encompassed only a small percentage of the working class, generally skilled workers. The AFL leadership of Samuel Gompers resisted efforts to alter this craft structure or initiate a drive to organize the masses of workers in basic industry. Moreover, many AFL unions barred Black workers from membership, or segregated them in separate locals; and the federation campaigned vigorously to shut off immigration from Asia and encouraged anti-immigrant chauvinism and racism.

The initial levies of U.S. communists, while divided among themselves on many organizational and some political questions, were in general agreement in rejecting political work by their members in the AFL. They openly advocated the federation's destruction.

Comintern leaders strongly disagreed with this position, and sought to convince U.S. communists to change it. In explaining their viewpoint, leaders of the International did not preclude that steps toward organizing the unorganized could develop outside AFL structures, nor that communists should participate in such efforts, and where appropriate even help initiate them. The most important existing arena for political work by U.S. revolutionists, however, was in AFL unions, which were far and away the country's largest labor organizations at that time. It was there that communists could win the broadest hearing for their ideas in the working class, combat the class-collaborationist strategy of the Gompers officialdom, project the need for mass unionization drives and independent labor political action, and fight to transform the unions into class-struggle instruments.

By 1921 most U.S. communists had been convinced on this question. The founding congress of the first united Communist Party in May of that year stated, "The Communist Party condemns the policy of revolutionary elements leaving" the AFL.[58]

Far from leading to a policy of ignoring the trade unions, the Bolsheviks' understanding of the relationship of imperialist superprofits, the labor aristocracy, and the labor bureaucracy helped equip the world communist movement with a sharper programmatic and strategic axis to guide genuine revolutionary activity in the labor movement. It helped them orient their primary attention toward the ranks, the masses of workers on the production line, the most oppressed and exploited layers in industry, the youth, the immigrants and oppressed nationalities, the women. The Theses on Tactics adopted by the third Comintern congress in 1921 explained:

> By descending into the most oppressed section of the proletariat, the Communist Parties are not championing one layer of the workers at the expense of others, but are furthering the interests of the working class as a whole. This the counterrevolutionary leaders have failed to do, preferring to advance the temporary interests of the labour aristocracy. . . .
>
> Those who promote the interests of the labour aristocracy, either counterposing or simply ignoring the interests of the unemployed, destroy the unity of the working classes and are pursuing a policy that has counter-revolutionary consequences.
>
> The Communist Party, as the representative of the interests of the working class as a whole, cannot merely recognize these common interests verbally and argue for them in its propaganda. It can only effectively represent these interests if it disregards the opposition of the labour aristocracy and, when opportunities arise, leads the most oppressed and downtrodden workers into action.[59]

Several things are noteworthy about this resolution, submitted to the Comintern by the Russian delegation. It identifies the Communist Parties as representatives of the working class *as a whole*, not of any particular section of the class, not even its most oppressed and exploited sections. It is in *that* capacity that communists must devote special attention to the interests of the most oppressed and exploited workers, because only by doing so can the true interests of the entire working class be advanced. In this regard, the resolution stresses that the bureaucracy serves only the *temporary* interests of the labor aristocracy, while the actual and enduring interests of all workers as a class are those advanced by the communists.

T̲HE BOLSHEVIKS'̲ understanding of the social roots of class-collaborationism also drove home the need for revolutionary workers, while actively participating in and seeking to provide leadership to struggles around the day-to-day issues in the factories, to combat every trace of a narrow, trade-unionist approach to communist tasks in the labor movement. The key to transforming the unions into the kind of class-struggle instruments capable of defending workers' interests, even at the shop-floor level, was to get labor to think socially and act politically. The unions had to see their function not only as defending the interests of their own members, but of advancing the goals of the entire working class and its oppressed and exploited allies at home and abroad.

Lenin perhaps put it best in the opening paragraphs of his theses on the agrarian question drafted for the second Comintern congress:

> Only the urban and industrial proletariat, led by the Communist Party, can liberate the working masses of the countryside from the yoke of capital and landed proprietorship, from ruin and the imperialist wars which will inevitably break out again if the capitalist system remains. . . .
> On the other hand, the industrial workers cannot accomplish their epoch-making mission of emancipating mankind from the yoke of capital and from wars if they confine themselves to their narrow craft, or trade interests, and smugly restrict themselves to attaining an improvement

in their own conditions, which may sometimes be tolerable in the petty-bourgeois sense. This is exactly what happens to the "labor aristocracy" of many advanced countries, who constitute the core of the so-called socialist parties of the Second International; they are actually the bitter enemies and betrayers of socialism, petty-bourgeois chauvinists and agents of the bourgeoisie within the working-class movement.

The proletariat is a really revolutionary class and acts in a really socialist manner only when it comes out and acts as the vanguard of all the working and exploited people, as their leader in the struggle for the overthrow of the exploiters.[60]

Trotsky and the Fourth International

Following the Stalinist degeneration of the Communist International between the mid-1920s and early 1930s, exiled Russian revolutionary leader Leon Trotsky led efforts to build a new world organization to carry on the fundamental programmatic and strategic tasks set out by the Comintern while Lenin had been alive. Among the political conquests incorporated in the program of the new Fourth International was the communist understanding of the role of divisions within the working class in general, and of the labor aristocracy in particular.

"Opportunist organizations by their very nature concentrate their attention on the top layers of the working class," explained the 1938 founding document of the Fourth International, the Transitional Program. "The sections of the Fourth International should seek bases of support among the most exploited layers of the working class," it said, pointing in particular to young workers and women workers.[61]

Trotsky discussed many of the questions dealt with above in an unfinished article he had been working on in August 1940 at the time of his assassination at the hands of Stalin's murder squad. The article, entitled "Trade Unions in the Epoch of Imperialist Decay," dealt with these issues in the context of the further evolution of imperialism since Lenin's time.

In 1940 fascism had triumphed throughout much of Europe, and the rival imperialist powers were plunging humanity headlong into a second worldwide carnage. Trotsky explained that to an even greater extent than twenty-five years earlier, monopoly capitalism had fastened its grip on the state apparatus at every level in the imperialist countries, and not only in those where fascism had triumphed. The labor movement had "to confront a centralized capitalist adversary, intimately bound up with state power," Trotsky wrote. He continued:

> Hence flows the need for trade unions—insofar as they remain on reformist positions, i.e., on positions of adapting themselves to private property—to adapt themselves to the capitalist state and to contend for its cooperation. In the eyes of the bureaucracy of the trade union movement, the chief task lies in "freeing" the state from the embrace of capitalism, in weakening its dependence on trusts, in pulling it over to their side.[62]

This is still the line promoted by the union officialdom in the United States, as they try to convince workers to hustle votes for Democratic Party "friends of labor" to counteract the "influence" of the "big-business lobby" in government.

Trotsky continued:

> This position is in complete harmony with the social position of the labor aristocracy and the labor bureaucracy, who fight for a crumb in the share of superprofits of imperialist capitalism. The labor bureaucrats do their level best in words and deeds to demonstrate to the "democratic" state how reliable and indispensable they are in peacetime and especially in time of war.[63]

Later in the article, Trotsky commented that, "all the efforts of the labor aristocracy in the service of imperialism cannot in the long run save them from destruction."[64]

Does this mean, Trotsky asked, that "the chief arena of work for revolutionists within the trade unions disappears"? Such a conclusion, he replied, "would be false to the core."[65]

> From what has been said, it follows quite clearly that, in spite of the progressive degeneration of trade unions and their growing together with the imperialist state, the work within the trade unions not only does not lose any of its importance but remains as before and becomes in a certain sense even more important than ever for every revolutionary party. The matter at issue is essentially the struggle for influence over the working class.[66]

Trotsky sought to emphasize the importance of these programmatic and strategic points to leaders of the Fourth International in the United States, particularly in relation to the question of the U.S. party's responsibility to conduct campaigns in industry for the rights of Black workers and of the entire oppressed Black nationality. Such efforts, Trotsky explained to several leaders of the U.S. Socialist Workers Party in 1939, "will bring a conflict with some white workers who will not want it." For the SWP, Trotsky stressed, these activities will mark a "shift from the most aristocratic workers' elements to the lowest elements."[67]

Trotsky explained that many radical middle-class supporters could be expected to part ways with the SWP as it continued to concentrate more of its attention and activity in the working class, as the party had voted to do at its founding convention the previous year. "Now that we are undertaking serious work," Trotsky said, "they are leaving us. I believe that we will lose two or three more strata and go more deeply into the masses. This will be the touchstone."[68]

THE U.S. REVOLUTIONISTS gave serious consideration to the points raised by Trotsky in his discussions with them. Stenographic transcripts of these discussions have been collected in the book *Leon Trotsky on Black Nationalism and Self-Determination*. That collection also contains two of the most important fruits of this political collaboration with Trotsky: "The SWP and Negro Work" and "The Right of Self-Determination and the Negro in the United States of North America," adopted by the July 1–5, 1939, convention of the Socialist Workers Party.

The first of these resolutions explained in its opening paragraph that, "Hitherto the party has been based mainly on privileged workers and groups of isolated intellectuals. Unless it can find its way to the great masses of underprivileged, of whom the Negroes constitute so important a section, the broad perspectives of the permanent revolution will remain only a fiction and the party is bound to degenerate."[69]

This remains a guiding principle for the Socialist Workers Party to this day.

In republishing major excerpts from Zinoviev's 1916 work on the "Social Roots of Opportunism," along with this historical review of the evolution of the important issues discussed by Zinoviev, *New International* hopes to contribute to efforts by revolutionary workers today to understand more clearly the continuing grip of class-collaborationist bureaucracies on the unions and mass workers parties, as well as the place of job trusts and other forms of the labor aristocracy, in the imperialist countries. It can help them understand why many workers support imperialist policies, why no labor party exists in the United States today, and why many workers—even where well-established labor parties do exist—still vote for even the most openly antilabor bourgeois politicians such as Britain's Margaret Thatcher. Such an understanding is part of the necessary preparation of workers' leaders for the fight to transform the labor movement.

The growth and changing national and sex composition of the working class in all imperialist countries; the onset of a worldwide economic crisis of capitalism in the early 1970s, which has brought austerity and greater insecurity for all working people; the political crisis of the imperialist system under the blows of revolutionary victories and struggles in Vietnam, Central America and the Caribbean, the Middle East, and Africa; and the combined impact of these changes on the consciousness of millions of workers and on their organizations—all this creates the greatest opportunities in decades for communists in the unions to win a wide hearing from their co-workers for a revolutionary alternative to the dead-end, class-collaborationist program and strategy of the current officialdom.[70]

NOTES

1. Olga Hess Gankin and H.H. Fisher (eds.) *The Bolsheviks and the World War* (Stanford: Stanford University Press, 1968), p. 59.

2. V.I. Lenin, "The Tasks of Revolutionary Social-Democracy in the European War" in *Collected Works* (hereafter cited as *CW*) (Moscow: Progress Publishers, 1974), vol. 21, p. 16.

3. Ibid., p. 18.

4. Lenin, "The War and Russian Social-Democracy" in *CW*, vol. 21, pp. 27–34.

5. Lenin, "The Position and Tasks of the Socialist International" in *CW*, vol. 21, pp. 40–41.

6. Lenin, "The Conference of the R.S.D.L.P. Groups Abroad" in *CW*, vol. 21, pp. 158–64.

7. Lenin, *CW*, vol. 22, p. 187.

8. Lenin, "Imperialism and the Split in Socialism" in *CW*, vol. 23, pp. 105–6.

9. Ibid., p. 110.

10. Ibid.

11. "The whole conception that the worker should *buy* his dwelling rests again on the reactionary basic outlook, already emphasised, of Proudhonism, according to which the conditions created by modern large-scale industry are morbid excrescences, and society must be brought forcibly, that is, against the trend which it has been following for a hundred

years, to a condition in which the old stable handicraft of the individual is the rule, and which, generally speaking, is nothing but an idealised restoration of small-scale enterprise, which has gone and is still going to rack and ruin. Once the workers are flung back into these stable conditions and the "social whirlpool" has been happily removed, the worker can naturally again make use of property in "hearth and home," and the above redemption theory appears less absurd. Proudhon only forgets that in order to accomplish all this he must first of all put back the clock of world history a hundred years, and that if he did he would turn the present-day workers into just such narrow-minded, crawling, sneaking servile souls as their great-great-grandfathers were." [Frederick Engels, "The Housing Question" in Karl Marx and Frederick Engels, *Selected Works* (Moscow: Progress Publishers, 1977), vol. 2, p. 316.]

12. Lenin, "Imperialism and the Split in Socialism" in *CW*, vol. 23, p. 114.

13. Lenin, "Debates in Britain on Liberal Labour Policy" in *CW*, vol. 18, pp. 360–69; "The British Labour Movement in 1912" in *CW*, vol. 18, pp. 467–68; "In Britain" in *CW*, vol. 19, pp. 55–56; "Harry Quelch" in *CW*, vol. 19, pp. 369–71.

14. Lenin, *CW*, vol. 23, p. 116.

15. "The Attitude to the 'Socialist' Currents and the Berne Conference" in *Theses, Resolutions and Manifestos of the First Four Congresses of the Third International* (hereafter cited as *Theses*) (London: Ink Links, 1980), p. 23. This translation has been checked against the original German text and revised.

16. Ibid., pp. 23–25.

17. Lenin, "The Collapse of the Second International" in *CW*, vol. 21, p. 247.

18. Marx and Engels, *Selected Works*, vol. 2, p. 82.

19. Marx, *Capital* (New York: Vintage Books, 1976), vol. 1, p. 135.

20. Ibid.

21. Marx, *A Contribution to the Critique of Political Economy*

(Moscow: Progress Publishers, 1970), p. 31.
22. Marx, *Capital*, vol. 1, p. 305.
23. Engels, *Anti-Dühring* (New York: International Publishers, 1976), p. 222.
24. Marx, *Grundrisse* (New York: Vintage Books, 1973), pp. 104–5.
25. Marx, *Capital*, vol. 1, p. 545.
26. Ibid., p. 305.
27. Marx and Engels, *Selected Correspondence* (Moscow: Progress Publishers, 1975), p. 222.
28. Ibid., p. 223.
29. Ibid., pp. 419–20.
30. Lenin, *CW*, vol. 22, p. 283.
31. Lenin, "How the Bourgeoisie Utilises Renegades" in *CW*, vol. 30, p. 34.
32. Marx and Engels, *Selected Works*, vol. 2, pp. 82–83.
33. Ibid., pp. 31–76.
34. Lenin, "What the 'Friends of the People' Are and How They Fight the Social-Democrats" in *CW*, vol. 1, pp. 299–300.
35. Lenin, *CW*, vol. 5, p. 400.
36. Ibid., p. 402.
37. Ibid., p. 412.
38. Ibid., p. 414.
39. Ibid., pp. 422–23.
40. Ibid., p. 426.
41. Lenin, *CW*, vol. 15, p. 38.
42. Lenin, *CW*, vol. 16, p. 347.
43. Ibid., p. 351.
44. Lenin, "The International Socialist Congress at Stuttgart" in *CW*, vol. 13, pp. 76–77.
45. Nick Salvatore, *Eugene V. Debs: Citizen and Socialist* (Urbana: University of Illinois Press, 1982), p. 245.
46. Lenin, "The International Socialist Congress at Stuttgart" in *CW*, vol. 13, p. 79.
47. Ibid., p. 81.

48. Lenin, "The Working Class and Its Press" in *CW*, vol. 20, p. 367.
49. Lenin, *CW*, vol. 21, p. 335.
50. Ibid., p. 310.
51. Marx and Engels, *Selected Works*, vol. 1, p. 167.
52. Lenin, *CW*, vol. 23, p. 120.
53. Ibid.
54. Lenin, *CW*, vol. 6, p. 489.
55. Lenin, *CW*, vol. 31, p. 50.
56. Ibid., pp. 52–53.
57. "The Communist International and the Red International of Trade Unions: The Struggle Against the Amsterdam (Scab) Trade-Union International" in *Theses*, p. 265.
58. Farrell Dobbs, *Revolutionary Continuity: Birth of the Communist Movement 1918–1922* (New York: Monad Press, 1983), p. 152.
59. *Theses*, p. 288. Checked against the German text and revised.
60. Lenin, "Preliminary Draft Theses on the Agrarian Question" in *CW*, vol. 31, pp. 152–53.
61. Leon Trotsky, *The Transitional Program for Socialist Revolution* (New York: Pathfinder Press, 1977), p. 151.
62. Trotsky, *Leon Trotsky on the Trade Unions* (New York: Pathfinder Press, 1975), p. 69.
63. Ibid.
64. Ibid., p. 72.
65. Ibid., p. 70.
66. Ibid., p. 71.
67. Trotsky, *Leon Trotsky on Black Nationalism and Self-Determination* (New York: Pathfinder Press, 1978), p. 66.
68. Ibid.
69. Ibid., pp. 71–72.
70. Leon Trotsky's unfinished August 1940 article on "Trade Unions in the Epoch of Imperialist Decay" also dealt with a question not discussed by Lenin or Zinoviev and not mentioned in the body of this article—i.e., the role of the labor

aristocracy in the colonial and semicolonial countries. Lenin concentrated on the imperialist countries, where the relative privileges of a minority of workers from monopoly superprofits made them a social base for the opportunist officialdom and its policies of support to its own capitalist exploiters, government, and the imperialist world system. Moreover, even at the time of Lenin's death in the early 1920s, the working class remained very tiny in almost all the oppressed countries, and the labor movement was barely in its infancy.

By the end of the 1930s, however, the continued export of capital by imperialism to a number of colonies and semicolonies and their increasing industrialization had created a still small but significantly larger and politically weightier working class in these countries. Unions and some working-class parties had been formed, but most of these quickly became bureaucratized and dominated by officials with a class-collaborationist perspective.

This superficial similarity with the labor movement in the imperialist countries, Trotsky pointed out, masked more important *differences*. The national capitalist class in the oppressed countries was weak and dependent on the imperialist monopolies; the young working class, while small, came onto the political scene with substantial power right from the outset. The political role of these workers and their organizations, even when dominated by a bureaucracy based on a layer of better-off workers, was very different from that of the opportunist-led labor movement in the imperialist countries.

While the labor bureaucracy in the United States or Britain, for example, served as a prop to perpetuate the world imperialist system, in the colonial countries it most often served as a social prop of sectors of the national capitalist class seeking more elbowroom and a bigger slice of the pie from monopoly capital. This class collaboration with local exploiters weakened the anti-imperialist struggle, which could only fully achieve its aims of national independence and development by a revolutionary political break from capitalist domination.

Nonetheless, the labor officialdom in the colonial world does not play a direct role as labor lieutenants of imperialist capital, as do the bureaucrats in the oppressor nations.

Trotsky put it this way in 1940:

"Inasmuch as the chief role in backward countries is not played by national but by foreign capitalism, the national bourgeoisie occupies, in the sense of its social position, a much more minor position than corresponds with the development of industry. Inasmuch as foreign capital does not import workers but proletarianizes the native population, the national proletariat soon begins playing the most important role in the life of the country. In these conditions the national government, to the extent that it tries to show resistance to foreign capital, is compelled to a greater or lesser degree to lean on the proletariat. On the other hand, the governments of those backward countries which consider it inescapable or more profitable for themselves to march shoulder to shoulder with foreign capital, destroy the labor organizations and institute a more or less totalitarian regime.

"Thus the feebleness of the national bourgeoisie . . . the pressure of foreign capitalism, and the relatively rapid growth of the proletariat, cut the ground from under any kind of stable democratic regime. The governments of backward, i.e., colonial and semicolonial, countries by and large assume a Bonapartist or semi-Bonapartist character; they differ from one another in that some try to orient in a democratic direction, seeking support among workers and peasants, while others install a form close to military-police dictatorship.

"This likewise determines the fate of the trade unions. They either stand under the special patronage of the state or they are subjected to cruel persecution. Patronage on the part of the state is dictated by two tasks that confront it: first to draw the working class closer, thus gaining a support for resistance against excessive pretensions on the part of imperialism; and, at the same time, to discipline the workers themselves by placing them under the control of a bureaucracy." [*Leon Trotsky on the Trade Unions,* pp. 71–72.]

Much more could be and needs to be said on this question, but that is not the purpose of this article. Suffice it to say that Trotsky's point about the relationship between bourgeois nationalist parties and governments and the labor bureaucracy based on a layer of privileged workers in the semicolonial countries is exemplified by the ruling Institutional Revolutionary Party (PRI) in Mexico and the large Peronist party in Argentina, which has been the government party there in the past. Both parties have a strong base of support in the officialdom of the organized labor movement in those countries.

The Chilean coup of 1973 is just one among many examples of the other option noted by Trotsky—where the dominant bourgeois sectors totally knuckle under to imperialism, seeking to crush the unions in the process.

As in the imperialist countries, the labor aristocracy in the oppressed nations forms a social basis for class-collaborationism and is less receptive to revolutionary solutions and Marxist organizations. Following the revolutionary victories in Cuba and Nicaragua, sections of these workers (e.g. among electrical workers in Cuba, construction and dock workers in Nicaragua), encouraged by the officials of their unions, pressed for excessive immediate wage increases, not recognizing the material limitations of the new governments and the need first of all to direct scarce resources to raising the conditions of the poorest layers of the working class and peasants. In some cases, the most bureaucratized and job trust–oriented unions have openly aligned with procapitalist opponents of the revolution, as is the case with several small unions in Nicaragua today.

Despite these problems, the Cuban and Nicaraguan leaderships have been generally successful in raising the political consciousness of most of these workers, eventually winning the leadership of their unions away from the opportunists and consolidating these workers as supporters of the revolution and its gains.

In the imperialist countries, the labor bureaucracy, based on a layer of "worker aristocrats," remains—as in the time of Lenin and Trotsky—a source of political support to the entire imperialist system that exploits and tyrannizes workers and farmers both in the oppressed and in the oppressor nations.

THE TEAMSTER SERIES BY FARRELL DOBBS
Lessons from the labor battles of the 30s

TEAMSTER REBELLION
The 1934 strikes that won union recognition for truckers and warehouse workers in Minneapolis and helped pave the way for the working-class social movement that built the industrial unions. The first of four volumes by a central leader of these battles.

TEAMSTER POWER
How the Teamster leadership used the power workers had gained during the 1934 strikes to make Minneapolis a union town and launch an 11-state campaign that brought tens of thousands of over-the-road truckers into the union.

TEAMSTER POLITICS
How Minneapolis Teamster Local 544 combated FBI and other government frame-ups in the 1930s, organized the unemployed, and fought to lead labor and its allies on an independent working-class political course.

TEAMSTER BUREAUCRACY
How class-conscious workers led labor opposition to US imperialism's entry into World War II. And how Washington, aided by the Teamster bureaucracy, used the FBI to try to smash union power and gag antiwar views. Now with more than 130 photos and illustrations.

Each volume $16. All volumes are available in Spanish.
Teamster Rebellion is also available in French, Farsi, and Greek.

WWW.PATHFINDERPRESS.COM

THE WORKING CLASS AND THE FIGHT FOR WOMEN'S EMANCIPATION

Women in Cuba: The Making of a Revolution Within the Revolution
VILMA ESPÍN,
ASELA DE LOS SANTOS,
YOLANDA FERRER

The integration of women in the ranks and leadership of the Cuban Revolution was intertwined with the proletarian course of the leadership of the revolution from the start. This is the story of that revolution and how it transformed the women and men who made it. $17. Also in Spanish, Farsi, and Greek.

Revolutionary Dynamics of Women's Liberation
GEORGE NOVACK

Explains why only a thoroughgoing reorganization of the entire social system—from the economic foundations to family relations—can eradicate the causes of women's inferior status. $5

The Emancipation of Women
V.I. LENIN

On women's equality. Including Clara Zetkin's interview with Lenin and a preface by N.K. Krupskaya. $7

Is Biology Woman's Destiny?
EVELYN REED

The roots of women's oppression as a "second sex." $5. Also in Farsi and Arabic.

Woman's Evolution
From Matriarchal Clan to Patriarchal Family
EVELYN REED

An expedition from prehistory to class society that reveals women's still largely unknown contributions to civilization. Pinpointing the historical factors that led to the subordination of women as a sex, Reed offers fresh insights on the struggle against their oppression and for the liberation of humanity. $25. Also in Farsi and Indonesian.

Women and the Family
LEON TROTSKY

How the October 1917 Russian Revolution, the first victorious socialist revolution, opened the door to new possibilities in the fight for women's liberation. $10

Sexism and Science
EVELYN REED

Are human beings innately aggressive? Does biology condemn women to remain the "second sex"? Taking up such biases cloaked as the findings of science, Reed explains that the disciplines closest to human life—anthropology, biology, and sociology—are permeated with rationalizations for the oppression of women and the maintenance of the established capitalist order. $15. Also in Farsi and Arabic.

Women and the Cuban Revolution
Speeches and Documents by Fidel Castro, Vilma Espín, and others

The victory of the Cuban Revolution, said Fidel Castro in 1966, "has meant a double liberation" for women, "who were discriminated against not only as workers but also as women." Includes the 1975 Family Code, documents of Cuba's Communist Party, and speeches by party leaders. $15

ARSENAL OF MARXISM

THE SOCIAL ROOTS OF OPPORTUNISM

by Gregory Zinoviev

The camp-followers

At the outbreak of the war the opportunists in the working class of all the most important countries became social chauvinists.[1]

The evolution of the individual persons, of the individual representatives of the Second International cannot be exhaustively explained in the light of the struggle of the two tendencies. It is not correct to maintain that *all* the present social chauvinists were previously opportunists. It is true beyond a doubt, however, that all the former opportunists are today social chauvinists. Individual, isolated exceptions merely prove the rule, in this case as well. The most important elements of modern social chauvinism were always latent in the old theory of opportunism. The war came, and everything that was still unclear in the ferment of opportunism took on sharply defined forms. The entire bourgeois residue which was until then concealed by the mask of socialism came suddenly out into the limelight. All the potential (bourgeois) energy took on kinetic form—what was kept secret until then was now openly expressed.

But here the question arises: where does opportunism in the socialist movement come from? How, by which path, and through which channels does this bourgeois influence penetrate the workers parties?

One of the causes of opportunism are the so-called camp-followers, that is, those strata of the electorate which are mainly recruited from the petty bourgeoisie, which do not belong to the Social Democratic Party and are not convinced socialists,[2] but nevertheless join with the social democracy occasionally under the influence of one accidental circumstance or another, contributing their voting strength in the elections.

This phenomenon has its deeper causes and is rooted, above all, in the entire development of the bourgeois parties and of bourgeois liberalism. In all countries in which—one way or another—a bourgeois revolution has taken place, the bourgeoisie has long been—in Germany, ever since 1848[3]—counterrevolutionary and inimical to the people. The historical experiences accumulated by the bourgeoisie have had their effect. Even in a country which is going through the state of development that present-day Russia is, the bourgeoisie has become a thoroughly counterrevolutionary factor.

Bourgeois liberalism has lost its attractive power and is continuing to lose it ever more, from year to year. In Germany, for instance, for some time now no genuine people's party has existed outside of the social democracy. There is no great bourgeois-democratic party to take into its ranks, not proletarians, but millions of the small people, those people who are dissatisfied with the existing order, who feel that they are at a disadvantage in modern society, who long for a radical economic and political improvement of their situation. All the dissatisfied, all the distressed, all the disfranchised elements are forced to go to the social democracy. No matter how moderate in its demands, how opportunistic the German social democracy was even before the war, it was the only democratic people's party in Germany. It alone defended, for better or for worse, the interests of the small people and the middle classes. Thus it became converted into a refuge for all the nonproletarian elements who could not stomach the practices of counterrevolutionary and antidemocratic liberalism, already fast in the grip of the imperialist claws. Under the influence of one or another aggressive measure on the part of the bourgeoisie or of the Junkers,[4] many hundreds of thousands of petty-bourgeois camp-followers came over and gave their votes to the social democracy.

THEREIN LAY the strength as well as the weakness of the German social democracy. Its strength consisted in the fact that the German social democracy had become the only people's party, that all the dissatisfied in the country sought its protection, that almost the entire democratic population flocked to its banner. Its weakness consisted in the fact that the petty-bourgeois camp-followers brought with them into the workers party the political lack of character, the indecision, the bourgeois mode of thinking, and all those other characteristics inherent in the strata that stand between the classes. Socialism became infected with opportunism.

In a country that has universal suffrage a particularly intensive vote-chasing is inevitable. In the chase after electoral successes, the German social democracy adapted itself to its eventual allies, to its camp-followers recruited among the nonproletarian strata. A whole category of people arose who voted for the social democracy, but only reluctantly joined the social democratic organization, who interested themselves exclusively in the general democratic and reformist work of the social democracy.

The world of the "camp-followers" also carried to the surface the corresponding leaders, Heine, Südekum, Landsberg, David—these are the typical representatives and leaders of such strata.[5] One such stratum, for instance, the innkeepers, is strongly represented in the social democratic fraction of the Reichstag.[6] Among the social democratic deputies to the Reichstag there were four innkeepers (out of 35 deputies) in 1892; six (out of 81) in 1905; twelve (out of 110) in 1912. Basing themselves upon the more backward layers of the working class, these ideological-political leaders of the camp-followers create a whole tendency inside the social democracy. Gradually a state within a state is formed. The petty-bourgeois influences grow constantly stronger. The social democracy itself becomes *a camp-follower of the camp-followers*. It is not the camp-followers who adapt themselves to the social democracy, but the social democracy that adapts itself to them. In the critical moments of history it is the petty-bourgeois and not the proletarian tendencies in the social democracy that win the upper hand. The petty bourgeoisie, due to its social situation, is doomed forever to vacillate between two camps. Thus it is not at all surprising that in the course of such a crisis as was created by the outbreak of the World War, the pendulum swung over to the bourgeois imperialist side and remained stationary there. That is how the bourgeoisie achieved a signal victory inside the German social democracy against the working-class elements.

Even in Germany's biggest cities, in the chief fortresses of the social democracy, more than a third of its voters do not belong to the working class, but to the bourgeoisie. To the petty bourgeoisie, for the greatest part; to those strata which are on their way toward proletarianization and stand close to the working-class population—but in any case, to the bourgeoisie. . . .

The German social democracy has its camp-followers not only in the big cities, however, but also in the countryside. In the elections of 1903 the votes cast *in the agricultural districts* were divided as follows among the various parties:

>   Center.............................. 1,033,051
>   Social Democratic Party........735,093
>   Conservatives 666,678
>   National Liberal Party..........546,216
>   Empire Party........................ 206,248
>   Liberal People's Party........... 174,122[7]

Thus the social democracy polled all of 735,093 votes in the elections of 1903 in the countryside alone. Undoubtedly the greatest part of these votes came from farm hands and day laborers. But even so, there can be no doubt that votes coming from the agrarian petty bourgeoisie are included in this total. The percentage of the latter is particularly low in the Catholic districts, but even in the Protestant districts it is not high.

By and large, the voters coming from bourgeois circles naturally only form a minority inside the German social democratic electorate. The majority of the social democratic voters consists of workers. (Among these, the better-situated workers, the so-called labor aristocracy, play a big role.) By the force of their numbers, the working-class element could impose their majority will upon the nonproletarian elements. But in reality this does not normally happen. The party *wants as many camp-followers as possible.* In practice, the party exerts all its energy to draw these bourgeois camp-followers to its side, not to do anything that might displease them very much. Consequently, a whole series of concessions to petty-bourgeois psychology, moderation of the proletarian demands, the opening of the road to opportunist unclarity.

Immediately after the abolition of the antisocialist laws, the German social democracy doubled its vote.[8] The total number of participants in the election fell in 1890 by almost 312,000 votes (1887, 7,540,900; 1890, 7,228,500). The number of social democratic votes, on the other hand, rose by some 664,200 votes (1887, 763,100; 1890, 1,427,300). Whoever followed German public affairs attentively could have observed even at that time, that this growth in the size of the vote was not simply due to the influx of many thousands of petty-bourgeois camp-followers. There was some talk, even then, about a certain kind of *coalition* between bourgeois democracy and the workers party.

As an indirect confirmation of this sort of evaluation of the events, the following simple but significant incident may serve. In 1891 the German social democracy considered it necessary to change its name. Previously the name was Social Democratic *Workers* Party of Germany. Now it is simply Social Democratic Party of Germany. The word "Workers" disappears from its name.

Obviously a social democratic workers party must not close its doors to people of another class origin. A social democratic party gathers within its ranks all those elements of society which adopt the point of view of the working class. But in its basic structure, it must remain a *workers* party. It can hardly be regarded as accidental that the German social democracy in the nineties considered it necessary to change its name precisely in the direction indicated. It must be assumed, moreover, that this was a manifestation of a decidedly opportunist tendency. In the light of the events of 1914, we are naturally inclined to become distrustful. There is even the danger that we might consider accidental and unimportant events retrospectively, as symptomatic of a whole line of opportunism. To all appearances, the incident we have cited has not, however—we repeat—been one of an accidental character.

Bebel disputes energetically the contention that the social democracy had become transformed from a socialist into just a democratic party.[9] The change in the name of the party, made in 1891, did not have the significance attributed to it, he contended. "Since the present writer," Bebel said, "proposed the new name, he is in the best position to furnish information as to the motives behind this proposal. Under the regime of the antisocialist law all sorts of 'socialisms' had made their appearance: in the bourgeois camp there was talk of Christian socialism, of government socialism—with special emphasis on the social insurance legislation—of conservative socialism, etc. It was necessary for us to distinguish ourselves clearly from all this. None dared to call themselves social democratic; therefore we chose the name social democracy, which, because of its brevity, had long before come into common usage."

That does not explain, however—we must remark for our part—why it was necessary to delete the word "Workers" from the name. Since such a decision could not have been made without weighing its political significance, it must be assumed that a definite political tendency was indeed inherent in this decision. The only question that remains is, what tendency? There can be no two opinions with regard to this: if there was any at all, it could only be an *opportunist* tendency.

We repeat: in the fact that a large number of "camp-followers" are beginning to penetrate the ranks of the German social democracy, we may perceive in a certain sense, not only a weak side, but also a strong side. Bebel was naturally correct in pointing out in his article that not only workers but all the needy and the suffering in general had to look for shelter in the social democracy. That is quite right, but the party must remain a *workers* party. And it must always underscore its proletarian character.

"The process of disintegration in bourgeois society," Bebel says,

> and the constantly more precarious situation of the middle and petty-bourgeois strata evoked by it, has also brought a change in the political structure of the bourgeoisie. New political parties have arisen which seek to represent the parliamentary interests of the socially threatened layers of the bourgeoisie. Such are the anti-Semitic and middle-class parties, for instance, who have constituted themselves an anti-Semitic fraction and an economic reform fraction in the Reichstag. The political party life of the bourgeoisie has thus become differentiated in accordance with its economic development. In the first place, this is to the disadvantage of the liberal parties, who have thus suffered the greatest losses among their following. But not by any means to the direct advantage of the social democracy. The latter has also suffered some losses, even if these cannot be proved by means of bare figures.

This is only one side of the process indicated by Bebel. Certain sections of the middle and petty bourgeoisie desert the party of the big bourgeoisie and form their own middle-class parties. But these intermediate parties have a more or less ephemeral existence in comparison with the new political parties.

The "new liberalism" of which the Marxists of the "Center" had been dreaming ever since 1910, did not come into being.[10] Democratic liberalism is impossible in a society which has reached such a maturity in its class relationships. The last few years of social development have proved the correctness of the views of Rosa Luxemburg and the whole left wing of German Marxism,[11] which had been carrying on a struggle against the alliance with the "new" liberalism.[12]

"Capitalism does not become more democratic, but constantly more plutocratic, and liberalism does not become more democratic but more reactionary," Bebel goes on to say.

A section of the middle and petty bourgeoisie aims at the creation of independent party combinations. But another—and very considerable—section joins the social democracy, strengthens it in the numbers of its voters and mandates, but weakens its socialist character.

MANY OF THESE CAMP-FOLLOWERS are not only poor socialists but also very inconsistent democrats. Many of them are shaky recruits, unreliable allies of the working class even in the purely parliamentary contests. Bourgeois demagogy—particularly that demagogy which rests upon a "patriotic" base—can always count upon a certain amount of success among these alleged adherents of social democracy. In this connection the official German social democracy was given a sound lesson by the elections of 1907.

These elections, which have gone down into political history as the "Hottentot Elections," took place under the sign of "patriotism."[13] Under the slogan of "saving the country," of strengthening the "military power" of Germany, of fighting for the "rightful interests of the nation" in the field of colonial policy, Prince Bülow succeeded in uniting all the bourgeois parties against the social democracy.[14] And by uniting their forces, these parties succeeded in administering an electoral defeat to the social democracy. The German social democracy lost 38 seats in parliament at the elections of 1907. To be sure, the absolute number of votes cast for the social democracy had risen by some 248,000. But the total number of voters participating in the elections had risen by about two million. In other words, *relatively* speaking, the German social democracy even lost votes in these elections.

THE PETTY-BOURGEOIS camp-followers of the social democracy had been taken in by the bait of "patriotism," and thus the opponents of the social democracy were assured of success. The workers received an imposing lesson. The dependence of the official German social democracy upon its camp-followers was distinctly proved.

Even on the eve of the elections, in January 1907, Franz Mehring had pointed out that Bülow and Company were intent on prying the camp-followers loose from social democracy with the aid of patriotic slogans.[15] . . .

Not only Mehring, but other German Marxists as well, were clearly aware of the fact that this dependence upon its camp-followers constituted the Achilles' heel of the social democracy. Just as clear was the knowledge that the petty bourgeoisie could most easily be ensnared with the aid of "national" questions.

In the first article in which the results of the "Hottentot Elections" were summed up, Kautsky explained the defeat of the German social democracy by the circumstance that the latter had underestimated the attractive power of the colonial idea in bourgeois circles. This defeat, he said, was administered to the social democracy by the middle strata which had deserted it this time. (K. Kautsky, "Der 25 Januar") Kautsky speaks of the loss of many hundreds of thousands of camp-followers from the middle strata, but he expresses the hope that they would soon return to the social democracy. In 1903, according to Kautsky, many peasants had voted for the social democracy. There has been no lack of elements originating from the nonproletarian strata, Kautsky tells us further, and he explains that he has in mind such elements among them as small businessmen, artisans, the new middle class, the government officials and office workers, physicians, teachers, engineers, etc. In concluding, Kautsky arrives at the reassuring result that the camp-followers are being absorbed gradually by the social democracy and that the social democracy must be the party of all the oppressed. We have gone into this argument more thoroughly in the above passages. Here it is important to establish the fact that Kautsky also admits the existence of *many hundreds of thousands* of social democratic voters originating from nonproletarian orbits of the population.

The outstanding parliamentarians and practical politicians of the German social democracy who at that time belonged to the Marxist camp also evaluated the outcome of the "Hottentot Elections" in more or less the same manner as the theoretician Kautsky. "The petty-bourgeois camp-follower has played a trick on us"—that is the general sense of this explanation. At the same time they cite figures which prove that this type of camp-follower has long been a powerful factor inside the German social democracy. . . .

In the elections of 1912 the camp-followers were once again on the side of the social democracy. On the one hand, they had become disillusioned with the policy of the bourgeoisie: the promises of mountains of gold had remained mere promises. The burdens of militarism were growing. Taxes were continually on the increase. The so-called financial reform brought about a deterioration in the condition of the middle class. On the other hand, for the official leaders of the Social Democratic Party the chief lesson of the elections consisted in this: *that it was necessary to adapt themselves even more to the camp-followers.* If the mountain refuses to come to Mohammed, Mohammed must go to the mountain.

As a result, we see in 1912 a new and very strong fluctuation of petty-bourgeois camp-followers toward the German social democracy. . . .

The leaders of German imperialism know exactly how dependent the German social democracy is upon its petty-bourgeois camp-followers. And they know very well how to play upon the chords of "patriotism."

Above all else the imperialist gentlemen would like to be assured of the demoralization of the workers, the main pillar of the German social democracy. In a book which appeared shortly before the outbreak of the war the well-known German imperialist, Rüdorffer (who is the active German diplomat, Rietzler), gives expression to the following sober views: "If international socialism should succeed in severing the worker, in his innermost convictions, from the structure of the nation and in making him a mere link of his class, then its victory is assured. For the purely violent means by which the national state can attempt to keep the worker fettered to itself must, by themselves and in the long run, prove to be entirely untenable. Should international socialism fail in this, however, and should those internal bonds which, even unconsciously, bind the worker to the organism known as the nation remain intact, then the victory of international socialism remains questionable as long as these bonds exist and turns into a defeat in case these bonds should, in the last analysis, prove to be the stronger."

THAT IS HOW THINGS STAND with regard to the workers. So far as the petty-bourgeois camp-followers are concerned, Mr. Rüdorffer sees no cause for worry. "When the government of Prince Bülow dissolved the Reichstag in 1907 over a question of colonial policy and appealed to the people, election experts, clinging to the experiences of previous days, regarded the electoral slogan as unpopular and held that a defeat was inevitable. The contrary happened. The older generation of politicians stood there, amazed at the elemental force of the nation's will to self-assertiveness in world politics," Rüdorffer-Rietzler tells us. Indeed, the patriotic propaganda of Bülow and his friends led to the most favorable results. The demagogic outcry about "defense of the fatherland," and "national interests," etc., exerted great influence over wide layers of the population. "No bourgeois party," writes Rüdorffer, "can permit itself a policy of negation in such questions; even the social democracy must, in its parliamentary conduct and in its agitation among the people, reckon with the national argument more and more each year." And several pages later, the same author says: "Even the social democracy, which bound by its program naturally remains in opposition, must exercise a certain amount of prudence and moderation in combating such demands and will not deny the fact that when such a question leads to new elections, it is sure to suffer a painful defeat."

Rüdorffer has observed the facts very correctly: out of the fear of losing its camp-followers, the official German social democracy has always made big concessions to petty-bourgeois "patriotism." "The election campaigns of the last few decades," the same author continues,

> have showed ever more distinctly that every emphasis upon the national questions by its opponents has reduced the attractive powers of the social democratic movement and that socialist agitation itself has been forced to conceal or to adulterate the international side of its program when facing its voters. . . . The party has been forced, in practice, to restrict its internationalism and to submerge it by means of all kinds of conditioning clauses. It has not dared to develop sharp agitational campaigns against any of the great armament budgets proposed in the past decade and its opposition to which it is theoretically obligated, has been conducted with a certain amount of prudence. It has indignantly denied the assertions of its opponents that in case of war, the social democracy will instigate the laboring masses following the party to turn their weapons against their leaders and thus seek to prevent the war together with the French socialists. Indeed, it even regards complaints of its lack of patriotism as insults. (Note that all this was written before the war—G.Z.)

The facts are here once again described correctly. The official German social democracy actually avoided an open struggle against bourgeois "patriotism." It took up the struggle against the bourgeoisie *on the latter's own premises*. The official opposition of the German social democracy on this question was exhausted by the thesis: "We are also patriots, we are even better patriots than you are." Instead of a struggle between two principles—internationalism against nationalism—there appeared an unprincipled rivalry over the question as to who the greater "patriots" were. And there can remain no doubt: *this position of the official German social democracy was determined in a very important measure by opportunist considerations as to how to hold the camp-followers to the party*. It suffices to recall the fact that in 1911 Molkenbuhr (one of the pillars of the party leadership and officially a "Marxist" and not an opportunist) proposed that the International Socialist Bureau should not be convoked and that no alarm should be sounded over the Morocco conflict.[16] He based this position upon the grounds that Reichstag elections were approaching in Germany and that it would not be favorable for the social democracy to have international politics debated at every election meeting and in every village in place of the questions of internal policy.

IMMEDIATE SUCCESSES in the elections, even if they had to be paid for at the price of concessions to national prejudice—that was always the aim of the opportunist wing of the German social democracy. The greatest possible number of seats in parliament—that is the Alpha and Omega of the policy of opportunism.

The old leaders of the social democracy attempted to combat this tendency which was steadily gaining the upper hand. But not always with success. On the eve of the elections of 1912 Bebel made a speech in Hamburg in which he postulated the following thesis: Let us rather have 50 deputies and 4 million votes than 100 deputies and 3 million votes. In other words: what is important for us is not the number of seats in parliament, but the number of sympathizers we have among the population. This was a feeble attempt to enter into a struggle against the policy of adaptation to the camp-followers. Only a feeble attempt; for, in order to speak out clearly it would have been necessary to say: let us rather have 2 million votes of *convinced socialists* than 4 million votes at the price of an adulteration of socialism; let us rather have twenty deputies who are really *socialists* than a hundred deputies of whom half are still deeply immersed in the petty bourgeoisie. But even for this feeble attempt Bebel was fiercely attacked by the opportunists. And to tell the truth, the elections of 1912 actually proceeded far more under the banner of Südekum than under that of old Bebel.

The opportunists began to demand ever more openly that the line of the social democracy be determined *not* by the party, not by the sum total of the *party* organization, but by all the *voters*. For while the party amounted altogether to about one million members, the voters on the other hand, numbered fully 4.5 million. "Our responsibility is toward broader masses," said the opportunists.

In 1912 the German social democracy consisted of 4,827 locals and over one million members—970,112 men and 130,371 women. For every hundred voters there were only 22.8 party members. "We," said the opportunists, "want to be responsible not only to these twenty-two but also to the other seventy-eight." In reality this meant that they wanted to free themselves of all responsibility, of *any kind* of discipline from the side of the organized socialist workers. In reality this meant that they considered themselves the political representatives *not of a revolutionary class, not of a revolutionary party, but of an accidental mass of petty-bourgeois camp-followers* who are radical today but fall into the arm of nationalism and reaction tomorrow, who vote for the social democracy today and tomorrow serve as tools of a robber imperialism.

Naturally, we do not wish to contend that the opportunism inside of the German social democracy arose only and exclusively because of the camp-followers. No, opportunism is the product of a whole series of facts. The camp-followers, however, constitute *one of the channels* through which opportunism penetrates the workers party.

The opportunists won the victory over the Marxists in the German social democracy and not in the German alone. *That signifies,* among other things, that the policy of adaptation to the petty-bourgeois camp-followers defeated the other policy. The official German social democracy has itself become a camp-follower, an agent, a tool of imperialism.

The labor bureaucracy

The term *"labor bureaucracy"* was long ago legitimized in scientific and political literature. When we spoke of labor bureaucracy before the war we understood by that almost exclusively the British trade unions. We had in mind the fundamental works of the Webbs,[17] the caste spirit, the reactionary role of the bureaucracy in the old British trade unionism, and we said to ourselves: How fortunate that we have not been created in that image, how fortunate that this cup of grief has been spared our labor movement on the continent!

But we have been drinking for a long time out of this very cup. In the labor movement of *Germany*—a movement which served as a model for socialists of all countries before the war—there has arisen just as numerous and just as reactionary a caste of labor bureaucrats. The present crisis has revealed this fact with unsparing clarity.

Up to now little has been known of the numerical composition of the labor bureaucracy, of its influence, of its income, of its corporative organizational strength. Just as a great many things are concealed from the public eye and wrought in secrecy within the circle of the leaders of the capitalist trusts, so it is in that closed caste of the labor bureaucracy which represents a unique job trust that directs the mass organization of the workers in all countries with an advanced labor movement. It is a characteristic attribute of every caste to be shut off from the entire world outside of it, to be accessible only to the initiated. That is why it is so extraordinarily difficult to obtain factual data about the role of the labor bureaucracy.

LET US FIRST OF ALL turn our attention to the labor movement in *Germany*. How strong is the labor bureaucracy there? How big is the influence of the "leaders" of the mass movement? Let us dwell for a while on the quantitative side of the matter. Several exceptionally interesting descriptions of the role of the labor bureaucracy, i.e., the role of the functionaries in the Social Democratic Party and in the free trade unions may be found in the *Handbuch des Vereins Arbeiterpresse* [Workers' Press Association Manual].[18] This manual has been appearing only for the past three years and is accessible only to functionaries of the labor movement. It cannot be obtained in bookstores. With great effort we succeeded in getting a copy of it for the purposes of this work. (We received this rare material on the situation of the German social democracy through the gracious aid of Comrade Julian Borchardt, to whom we express our thanks here.)

At the very end of the booklet there is an alphabetical index of all the paid officials working for the party and the free trade unions. This register of names alone occupies twenty-six pages of three columns each in print of the very smallest petit type. According to our calculation, the entire number of paid officials working for the party and the trade unions in 1914 amounts to 4,010. In Greater Berlin alone it amounts to 751, in Hamburg to 390. . . .

In general the picture is the same all over. The great, the overwhelming majority of the functionaries are *workers*. The purely bourgeois elements (merchants, academicians, literary men, etc.) is strongest in the opportunist center, Munich, and in part also in Frankfurt and Stuttgart. Generally, however, it may be said that workers constitute the absolutely preponderant element among the "upper" four thousand functionaries of the German labor movement. This fact cannot be disputed and in this respect our data here corresponds with all the other data.

But the concept "worker," in and of itself, must be applied with the greatest care in this case. It would be better perhaps in this case not to say "worker" but "worker in his origin." For such party leaders as Scheidemann, Ebert, Legien, Pfannkuch, etc., also belong in the category of worker-functionaries.[19] Scheidemann is a compositor, Ebert a saddler, Legien a turner, Pfannkuch a carpenter, Molkenbuhr a tobacco worker. In reality, however, these people are no longer workers and have not been for decades. They have incomes bigger than that of the average bourgeois and have long ago given up their trades.[20] They are workers in the same sense as the well-known "labor" ministers John Burns, Henderson, Fisher, etc.[21] And that holds true not only for people in the center who stand on the highest rung of the bureaucratic ladder and direct all the affairs, like Legien, Scheidemann, etc. It holds true also for the *great majority of all the four thousand functionaries of the German labor movement.* In the provinces the picture is the same, the functionaries have long ago given up their original trade. They are workers in name only. In reality they are bureaucrats with a standard of living quite distinct from that of the average worker.

The worker-functionaries very often hail from the circles of the labor aristocracy. The labor *bureaucracy* and the labor *aristocracy* are blood brothers. The group interests of the one and of the other very often coincide. Nevertheless, labor bureaucracy and labor aristocracy are two different categories. (The role of the latter has a special subchapter devoted to it.) . . .

According to our calculation, four thousand functionaries occupy at least twelve thousand—if not more—important party and trade union functions. Every more or less efficient functionary takes care simultaneously of two to three and often even more offices. He is at the same time a Reichstag deputy and an editor, a member of the Landtag [regional parliament] and a party secretary, the president of a trade union, an editor, a cooperative functionary, a city councilman, etc. Thus all power in the party and trade unions accumulates in the hands of this upper four thousand. (The salaries accumulate, too. Many of the officials of the labor movement receive ten thousand marks and over per year.[22]) The whole business depends upon them. They hold in their hands the whole powerful apparatus of the press, of the organization, of the mutual-aid societies, the entire electoral apparatus, etc.

At the moment in which we are setting down these figures, a report has come in of the death of the outstanding Hamburg social democrat, Adolf von Elm. In the obituaries all the offices von Elm held in the last years of his life are enumerated. We have counted a dozen and a half such offices in trade union and cooperative organizations. Reichstag deputy, chairman of the press commission, member of the social democratic fraction of the city council, chairman of the district committee of the Wholesale Buying Association, etc., etc.—these are some of his offices. And von Elm is by no means an exception.

R**EGARDING THE NUMBER** of persons vested with functions and of "representatives" in the individual provincial organizations of the Social Democratic Party, there is very little material in the press. There are some isolated examples, however, which are noteworthy. Thus, for instance, the social democratic organization of the Baden district had 7,322 members all told in 1905; its representatives in the municipalities, however, reached a figure well above the thousand mark. Consequently, every seventh party member in Baden was, in a certain sense, a party functionary.

But the real power in the party does not reside in the hands of the relatively broad layer of "representatives." It rests in the hands of a much smaller stratum of party functionaries, the top bureaucracy. More than a thousand small employees, clerks, managers, etc., are directly dependent economically upon the party and trade union leadership. As early as 1904 there were already 1,476 men in the employ of the printshops belonging to the Social

Democratic Party (the number of editors had reached 329). In 1908, 298 men worked in the *Vorwärts* plant alone. All these people are just as dependent economically upon the higher bureaucrats as the workers are on any given private entrepreneur. . . .

The *Vorwärts* alone is a great enterprise that feeds several hundred party functionaries and employees. It was upon these functionaries, above all, that the party leadership (Scheidemann and Co.) supported themselves when they seized possession of the *Vorwärts* with the aid of the government, at the end of 1916, violating the legal prerogatives of the oppositional Berlin organization.[23] It was upon these functionaries that the party leadership supported itself also in Bremen, Stuttgart, and a number of other cities when they wrested from the oppositional majority the local newspapers, the publishing houses and bookstores, the treasuries, etc., with methods of brutal force. The legal owner of the party property is in most cases some party functionary. If the majority of workers in any locality oppose the party leadership, the legal owner appeals, with Scheidemann's blessings, to the "law." The editors who permit an expression of the views of the opposition are discharged after being paid their salaries for six weeks in advance and—suddenly the paper becomes "patriotic." The reactionary role of the labor bureaucracy is so openly revealed in such cases as to leave nothing more to be desired.

The youth organizations brought a breath of fresh air into this set-up. Here there was no stultifying routine. These organizations enjoyed organizational autonomy on a genuinely democratic basis. A spirit of equality and brotherliness prevailed. Every tendency toward bureaucratism was eschewed. And what happened? Hardly ten years passed before the official party (the "adults") succeeded in penetrating the youth committees as well with its bureaucrats.

Naturally the youth organizations never thought of refusing well-meant aid from the side of the adult "Marxists"; on the contrary, they valued it greatly. But the "party heads" did not restrict themselves to that. They wanted to get into their hands the entire apparatus of the youth organizations. For the youth are notoriously an "unreliable" band of enthusiasts. And by systematic efforts the "older" generation of opportunists succeeded completely in achieving their aim. Inside the responsive social democratic youth of Germany, in a state of continual ferment, an almost unanimous *opposition* against the official course has prevailed. But the official youth paper and the official youth committees stand entirely and completely behind Scheidemann and Company. The "adult" bureaucrats have done their "duty" to the "party." Wherever the youth has attempted, in the course of the war, to defend the autonomy of its organization, it has been deprived of its means of existence; the party subsidies have been withdrawn, they have been kicked out of the headquarters, the "People's Houses," in which they have been lodged. Finally, the recalcitrant organizations were dissolved altogether. That is what has recently happened in Hamburg, for instance, one of the great centers of the German labor movement. . . .

THE TRADE UNIONS CITE, in their literature, detailed data regarding the moneys required for the maintenance of the bureaucracy in the trade unions. In 1914 alone the administrative costs of the free trade unions of Germany reached the round sum of 12,877,090 marks. These administrative costs are in the greatest part expenses for the maintenance of functionaries, because all the other categories of expenditures—such as those for agitation, educational purposes, etc.—are *entered separately*. Thus it appears that expenses for the maintenance of the trade union bureaucracy and several other administrative expenditures together amount to 13 million marks annually, consequently to *over one million monthly*. The lion's share of these sums is spent directly on the salaries of the trade union functionaries. This is apparent from the figures of the expenditures incurred by the central administration of the free trade unions. Here the expenditures for salaries are quoted separately. Of the 2,009,834 marks constituting administrative costs, the salaries, the personal administrative costs, amount to 1,266,615 marks.

THE TOTAL SUM of all expenses paid out by the free trade unions in 1914 amounts to 79,547,272 marks. Of these 80 million, 12 million marks were spent in one year (1914) for agitation, maintenance of connections, etc., and 2,598,476 marks for educational purposes. Here we have again twelve and a half million marks, of which a good part was likewise spent for personal salaries due to speakers, journalists, etc. These twenty-five million, which are expended annually for administration, agitation, etc., are of course collected by more than one thousand trade union functionaries who form a closed group.

We cite below the latest data regarding the number of functionaries in the free trade unions of Germany. These data were made public in October 1916. In forty-six trade unions—it is still only the free (social democratic) trade unions that are in question—the following number of functionaries were employed in 1914, before the outbreak of the war:

> In the Central Offices 407
> In the District Offices 429
> In the Local Unions 1,956
> In the Editorial Offices of the
> Trade Union Papers.................. 75
> Total... 2,867

Toward the end of 1914 this figure dropped to 2,287; toward the end of 1915 to 1,477. The war had cut the number of functionaries down to half the previous figure. But the *prewar* figure must naturally be taken as the normal figure. Thus almost 3,000 paid officials—chairmen, presidents, editors, etc.—are employed by the German free trade unions.

In 1915—right in the middle of the war—the costs of the central administration of the German free trade unions amounted to 1,718,820 marks. The expenses are divided into two categories: for materials, and for personnel. The former amounted to 488,389 marks in 1915; the latter, i.e., the functionaries' salaries in the first place, to 1,230,431 marks. And that only in the central administration! Together with the expenses of the local departments, the administrative costs in 1914 amounted to 9,721,190 marks, i.e., almost ten million.

The publication of the trade union organs—a separate category—cost 2,079,049 marks (circulation 2,610,695) in 1914, and 1,225,165 marks (circulation 1,328,218) in 1915. Obviously, a good part of these sums is expended on salaries received by trade union officials, editors, editorial secretaries, permanent staff workers, etc.

These sums are enormously high!

In the Social Democratic Party as well as in the free

trade unions there has been a notably over-developed *specialization of functions*—an extremely favorable circumstance for the labor bureaucracy. Hundreds of labor bureaucrats specialize in communal policy, in insurance problems, in the consumers' cooperative system, etc. In the social democratic Reichstag fraction the division of labor among the speakers according to professional specialities has taken on extreme forms. In the trade union movement the situation is the same. A whole science of bureaucracy—if one may say so—has arisen. The statutes of the German Metal Workers Federation, for instance, fill 47 printed pages and 39 paragraphs, of which each is once again subdivided into ten to twelve sections. That is really a complete bureaucratic encyclopedia. The uninitiated inevitably go astray in the midst of it. Only a specialist, a functionary who has been engaged in such affairs for years, can find his way in it without trouble.

THE GOOD OLD German social reformists are very much concerned that the social democracy shall have "sufficiently trained" leaders, that the functionaries of the labor movement shall be up to the "necessarily high level" of their tasks. The bourgeois professor, Ferdinand Tönnies (today an open imperialist) proposes that the Social Democratic Party should introduce regular examinations. Before a party member can become a candidate in the election, or for a secretarial post, he should be obliged to pass an examination.

The well-known Prof. Heinrich Herkner goes even further. He poses the question as to whether the great trade union federations can content themselves altogether with leaders of working-class origin. He foresees a situation in which the trade unions will soon be compelled to do without exclusively proletarian elements and to prefer as directors, persons who possess economic, juridical, and commercial school training. That means nothing else than that the workers are being propositioned with the idea of choosing for themselves educated bourgeois as leaders, of selecting their functionaries from the ranks of the *bourgeois* intelligentsia "standing above the party." And this proposition is not at all unexpected if we recall the usages in the labor movement of other advanced countries. In England, for instance, the socialist paper, *Daily Citizen*, founded by the trade unions, not so long ago selected its editors from among the staff of the bourgeois *Daily Mail*. The *Daily Citizen*, could not, or did not want to, find sufficiently experienced journalists among the socialist writers. The paper was organized on the model of the "great" European newspapers. Inside of a very short time it ate up a million marks and went under. This is a very characteristic picture of the practices prevalent in these spheres. . . .

The reactionary role of the trade union bureaucracy is confirmed even by such moderate critics as the historians of the British trade union movement, the Webbs. But we cannot here go into the role of the labor bureaucracy in England more thoroughly (the number of *top* functionaries in the trade unions in 1905 was 1,000; more recent figures are, unfortunately, not available). That would be too much of a digression.

In the land of "unlimited possibilities," in America, the leaders of the labor unions sell themselves quite openly to the bourgeoisie. There the material dependence of the leaders upon the bourgeoisie is not even concealed. There it is a common practice for the capitalists and labor leaders, and their respective wives, to exchange valuable "gifts" after the conclusion of a wage agreement with the trade unions. Naturally, this is quite ordinary bribery. The labor leaders there are often pure and simple handymen of the bourgeoisie, "labor lieutenants of the capitalist class," as they say in America. That is no longer a matter of petty-bourgeois hangovers or of the group interests of the labor aristocracy, but plain and ordinary venality. There, the trade unions do a wholesale and retail trade with labor votes before the presidential elections. The leaders of the labor unions over there take a prominent part in various capitalist associations.

One example: the notorious Samuel Gompers. He is simultaneously the president of the American Federation of Labor, that is, the trade union federation of the workers; and first vice-president of the Civic Federation, that is, the most important capitalist organization for the combating of socialism. When Gompers came to Europe in 1909, Karl Kautsky extended to him this mocking greeting: "Welcome, brother—president of the American labor unions; begone, Mr. Vice-President of the National Federation of American capitalists!"

However, the reactionary role of the "socialist bureaucracy" appears nowhere so ostentatiously as in Australia, that veritable Land of Promise of social reformism. The first "labor ministry" in Australia was formed in Queensland in December 1899. And ever since then the Australian labor movement has been a constant prey of leaders on the make for careers. Upon the backs of the laboring masses there arise, one after another, little bands of aristocrats of labor, from the midst of which the future labor ministers spring forth, ready to do loyal service to the bourgeoisie. All these Holmans, Cooks, and Fishers were once workers.[24] They act the part of workers even now. But in reality they are only agents of the financial plutocracy in the camp of the workers.

The caste of the "leaders" here appears quite openly as a unique type of job trust. The labor party as such comes to the surface only during the parliamentary elections. Once the elections are over, the party disappears again for three whole years. The party conventions are only conventions of party functionaries. They never include a trace of real representatives of the mass of labor. The party leader is elected in conference and functions as such until the next election at the succeeding conference. If he is elected to Parliament, he also becomes the leader of the parliamentary fraction. If the party gets a majority in Parliament, the leader becomes prime minister and forms a "labor ministry." The powers of this leader are almost unlimited. It went so far that the "labor" minister of New South Wales, Holman (a former carpenter), proposed at the party conference of 1915 that the leader be given the power to change the *program of the party* at his own discretion, if this should be necessary for its "salvation." We have recently had quite a striking example of the means whereby Fisher, Holman, and Company "save" the labor party. These "leaders" have proved to be the worst sort of chauvinists. The majority of the workers pronounced themselves against the introduction of military service in Australia. But Fisher and his friends continue to represent the views of the bourgeoisie.

When the Danish socialist, Stauning, not so long ago became a minister, Huysmans congratulated him on his success and noted with joy the fact that Stauning is the tenth socialist to become a minister.[25] It would be interesting to know whether Huysmans counts Fisher also among the ten ministers.

There is one consolation for the opponents of Fisher,

nevertheless. Namely, that even in distant Australia it has come to an open break between Fisher and the genuine labor organizations. "Every cloud has its silver lining." The present crisis has accentuated the situation tremendously and it will lead to a good and healthy "cleansing" of the democratic ranks.

THE MOST FAR-SIGHTED of the German reactionaries knew long before the war that the official organizations of the German social democracy had become thoroughly "bourgeoisified." And they said quite openly that at the critical moment they would appeal to the leaders, to the heads of the Social Democratic Party against *the laboring masses*. . . .

Naturally, the socialists long ago recognized the reactionary role of the labor bureaucracy, but not quite so clearly as they did after the salient lesson of August 4, 1914. One of the leaders of the German trade union movement, the chairman of the bookbinders' union, once declared quite openly and honestly before a conference of the trade union leadership, not so much as a complaint but rather as a self-evident fact, that he had to say that all those present were much more interested in the establishment of a new system of society when they were still on the workbench and had to be content with low wages, than they were now. The minutes carry a notation on this point, that the speaker was interrupted with numerous heckles directed against the opinion he expressed. But one particular heckler called out from his seat: "That is even far more true of the party functionaries."

Wilhelm Liebknecht was fully conscious of the fact that the labor aristocracy predominated among the party leaders.[26] "You who sit here," he once turned to say to the delegates at a party convention, "are also, most of you, aristocrats, to a certain extent, among the workers—I mean insofar as incomes are concerned. The laboring population in the mining regions of Saxony and the weavers in Silesia would regard such earnings as yours as the income of a veritable Croesus." August Bebel often underscored the change of mentality among the leaders once they have attained the living standard of the bureaucracy, of the officialdom, of the aristocrats of labor. At the Dresden convention of the party Bebel said that the majority of the party functionaries were people who considered the positions attained by them as, in some way, the culmination points of their careers. . . .

In 1911 Robert Michels, a former member of the social democracy and today a "socialist" professor in Turin, published a book under the title *The Sociology of the Party Structure in Modern Democracies*. [The English edition is titled *Political Parties*.] His investigation is confined mainly to facts in the life of the German social democracy. The author has no uniform view of his own. He vacillates back and forth between vulgar reformism and quasi-revolutionary syndicalism. Many of his generalizations are often premature and cannot stand up against even feeble criticism. Thus, for instance, the author tends to hold the absolutely false conception that the emergence of a putrefied upper bureaucratic stratum is an inevitable phenomenon in every democracy. The author believes, in his fatalism, that this phenomenon is inherent in *the essence of democracy itself*. But his observations, and the material which the author has collected, are of great interest.

Michels has graphically described the rule of the upper bureaucratic stratum over the entire mass of members and followers of the German social democracy in the following manner:

- Committees
- Functionaries
- Attendance at membership meetings
- Party members
- Voters

The base of this pyramid is formed by the mass of four million social democratic voters. Then follows the still quite numerous stratum of party members, numbering close to a million. After that, those who attend the membership meetings, a considerably smaller number. Above them stands a small group of party functionaries, and the top of the pyramid is constituted, finally, by the narrow caste of *the most important party* functionaries—the committees.

Thus the powerful apparatus that exerts such a tremendous influence on the course of affairs in the German social democracy lands in the hands of the committees, i.e., stands uncontrollably at the disposal of an oligarchic group of a few thousand officials.

The well-known Dutch Marxist, Anton Pannekoek, who was active for a long time in the ranks of the German social democracy,[27] has characterized the present situation of the party as follows:

> The German social democracy . . . is a firmly established, gigantic organization, which exists almost as a state within the state, with its own officials, with its own finances, its own press; within a certain spiritual sphere of its own, with an ideology all its own. . . . The entire character of this organization is suited to the peaceful

preimperialist epoch. The human agents of this character are the functionaries, the secretaries, the agitators, the parliamentarians, the theoreticians, who form a caste of their own, a group with separate interests, which dominates the organizations both materially and ideologically.

It is no accident that all of them, with Kautsky at their head, wanted to have nothing to do with a real *struggle* against imperialism. Their whole interest in life is of a nature inimical to the new tactic, a tactic which endangers their existence as functionaries. Their quiet work in the offices and in the editorial chambers, in conferences and in council or committee meetings, in the writing of erudite and not so erudite articles against the bourgeoisie and against one another—all this peacefully businesslike activity is being threatened by the storms of the imperialist epoch. . . . This whole bureaucratic scholarly apparatus . . . can only be saved by being removed outside the bounds of this boiling pot, outside of the revolutionary struggle, outside of the real, the main stream of life (and consequently into the service of its own bourgeoisie—G.Z.).

If the party and the leadership were to adopt the tactic of mass action, the state power would immediately swoop down upon the organizations—the basis of their entire existence and of all their activity in life—and perhaps destroy them, confiscate their treasuries, arrest the leaders, etc. Naturally, it would be an illusion to believe that the power of the proletariat can thus be broken: the organizational power of the workers resides not in the form of their group associations, but in the spirit of solidarity, in discipline, in unity;

by these means the workers could create better forms of organization. But for the functionaries that would mean the end, for the particular organizational form is their entire world, without which they could not exist or function. The urge toward self-preservation, the group interests of their craft, must of necessity force upon them the tactic of avoiding a struggle with, and of giving way to, imperialism. (Anton Pannekoek, "Der Imperialismus und die Aufgaben des Proletariats," [Imperialism and the Tasks of the Proletariat] in *Verbote, Internationale Marxistische Rundschau,* January 1916.)

Of course, all this must not be over-simplified. *Objectively* the labor bureaucracy—the so-called leaders—betrayed the cause of the workers in Germany on August 4. And not only in Germany. But that must not be taken to mean that every one of these leaders said to himself at the decisive moment: I had better go over to the side of the bourgeoisie, else I am going to lose my bread and butter, my position in public life, etc. Not at all! *Subjectively,* many members of this caste are still convinced to this day that they have been acting exclusively in the interests of the working class, that their conduct was dictated by their better understanding of the proletarian interests. When we speak of the "treachery of the leaders" we do not mean to say by this that it was all a deep-laid plot, that it was a consciously perpetrated sell-out of the workers' interests. Far from it. But consciousness is conditioned by existence, not *vice versa.* The entire social essence of this caste of labor bureaucrats led inevitably, *through the outmoded pace set for the movement in the "peaceful" prewar period,* to complete bourgeoisification of their "consciousness." The entire position into which this numerically strong caste of leaders had climbed over the backs of the working class made of them a social group which objectively must be regarded as an agency of the imperialist bourgeoisie.

In his dispute with the leader of the opportunists, von Vollmar, Bebel repeatedly pointed out that the social position of the former (von Vollmar belonged to the upper strata and was fabulously rich) prevented him from understanding the griefs of the working class and *therefore made him into an opportunist* tending toward a nationalistic, liberal policy.[28] Although this may not always be true in the case of an individual person (an individual can raise himself above the milieu of his class, above his social group), it is absolutely true for the entire social stratum of the labor bureaucracy.

THE RISE OF AN ENTIRE, numerically strong stratum of labor bureaucrats—as well as the mass influx of electoral camp-followers—is, at one and the same time, a symptom of strength as well as of weakness in the labor movement. Of strength—because it testifies to the *numerical* growth of the movement. An organization with only a few thousand members can get along without paid functionaries. When it begins to have hundreds of thousands and millions of members it necessarily needs a big and complex organizational apparatus. But the rise of this stratum becomes a symptom of weakness in the movement when the leaders of the workers' organizations degenerate into officials in the worst sense of the word, when it begins to lack the broad proletarian impetus necessary to the given stage of development. Every people, so the saying goes, has the kind of government it deserves. This can be amplified by adding that every labor movement also has the kind of leadership it deserves.

At the time of the crisis on the eve of the war, the labor bureaucracy played the role of a reactionary factor. That is undoubtedly correct. But that does not mean that the labor movement will be able to get along in the future without a big organizational apparatus, without an entire stratum of people devoted especially to the service of the proletarian organization. We do not want to go back to the time when the labor movement was so weak that it could get along without its own employees and functionaries, but rather to go forward to the time in which the labor movement itself will be something different; in which the stormy movement of the proletariat will subordinate the stratum of functionaries to itself; in which routine will be destroyed, bureaucratic corrosion wiped out; which will bring new men to the surface, infuse them with fighting courage, fill them with a new spirit.

The group of the "leaders" has dealt a heavy blow to the cause of the workers. Not only those labor leaders who hail from the bourgeoisie but also those who hail from the working class, who were elected by the workers and who owe their positions to working-class democracy. That is undoubtedly true. But that does not mean that the idea of democracy has therefore collapsed. . . .

THE POISONOUS WEED of labor bureaucracy grew on the soil of the "peaceful" epoch, not because of, but despite, the democratic organization. Only opportunism—a form of expression corresponding to this epoch—and not the democratic organizational principle, has suffered bankruptcy. New times will come and we shall hear new songs. As soon as the masses themselves enter the historical arena they will put an end to the uncontrollable labor bureaucracy. The coming new epoch will bring forth a new generation of leaders and new forms of control on the part of the working masses over their deputies and plenipotentiaries.

We do not at all wish to contend that the entire crisis can be explained by the treachery of the leaders. The treachery of the leaders in itself can only be explained by more profound causes inherent in the epoch. But not everything can be unshouldered on this epoch. The fact of the betrayal by the leaders must not be passed over in silence. Treachery has been committed. It is necessary to call things by their name. It is our task not only to explain the causes of opportunism but also to *combat* opportunism. It is our duty not only to trace down the causes of the "treachery," but also to unmask the traitors and to render them harmless. The betrayal by the official leaders of the German social democracy, the counterrevolutionary role of the party and trade union bureaucracy during the war, was so infamous that in the periodical of the people forming the social democratic "center," in the *Neue Zeit* of 1916, may be found such lines as the following, the pen products of Kautsky's co-thinker, the lately deceased Gustave Eckstein: "The leaders were constrained to remain radical in words, in order to hold the masses behind them. In actuality, however, they aimed in the immediate period to obtain petty reforms which, however, could not be gotten without great struggles. Out of habit the leaders developed an 'oracular smile.' The organization became more and more of an end in itself, which ever more and more dislodged the thought of achieving the final goal from their heads and from their hearts."

After two years of war the honest representatives of the "center" also had to admit that the present official organization of the German social democracy had become a counterrevolutionary factor, that the leaders had become "oracles." That is exactly what Rosa Luxemburg had said in her polemics against Kautsky as far back as 1912.

Robespierre in his time attempted to differentiate between *representatives* of the people (*"représentants du peuple"*) and *plenipotentiaries* of the people (*"mandataires du peuple"*).[29] Representation of the people, in his opinion, cannot be realized: "Will cannot be represented" (*"la volonté ne peut se représenter"*). Robespierre recognized only *plenipotentiaries* of the people. The plenipotentiaries of the people carry out the mandate given them by the people.

The caste of opportunist leaders of the labor movement still consists today, unfortunately, of formally recognized "representatives" of the working class. But in its essence this caste has become the tool of an enemy class. The members of this caste who formally possessed full power in the working class are in reality *the emissaries of bourgeois society in the camp of the proletariat.*

Opportunism and the labor aristocracy

Until very recently the question of the labor aristocracy and its conservative role in the labor movement has been treated as a problem almost unique to the *British* labor movement. The epoch of the latest form of imperialism and the events in the labor movement of the entire world in connection with the World War have posed this question on a much wider scale. It has become one of the most basic questions of the labor movement *in general*. The victory of opportunism and social chauvinism in Germany—and not in Germany alone—is intimately bound up with the victory of the narrow, group interests of the relatively small group of labor aristocrats over the genuine interests of the many-millions-strong laboring mass, which constitutes *the working class.*

For many years England was the Promised Land of bourgeois influence upon the proletariat and consequently the Promised Land of the opportunists. It has become commonplace in socialist literature to recognize this circumstance as being conditioned by the monopolistic position of England on the world market. The surplus profit which the British bourgeoisie has derived thanks to this monopolistic position, has enabled it to bribe "its" workers and thereby to tear them loose from the socialist movement. But it would be false to believe that the magnanimity of the British capitalists was extended in equal measure to the entire working class. No, with these crumbs they bought off mainly the upper stratum of the working class—the labor aristocracy. That sufficed in order—under otherwise favorable conditions for the bourgeoisie—to demoralize the British labor movement.

Among the great masses of the *unskilled* proletariat indescribable poverty prevails even in England. Their condition has not been much better than the condition of their brothers in other countries. Even in the heyday of British capitalism there were in England considerable strata of unskilled workers who lived in circumstances not much better than those described by Frederick Engels in his *The Condition of the Working Class in England.*

In one of his well-known works, published in 1902 (*The Social Revolution*), Kautsky deals with the economic conditions of the working class in England in the second half of the nineteenth century. He distinguishes clearly between the minority of the skilled, and the majority of the unskilled, workers. Kautsky analyzes the tables compiled by the bourgeois economist, E.L. Bowley, who contends that in the thirty years between 1860 and 1891 the wages of the British workers rose by 40 percent (the reference is to *nominal wages*) and he comes to the conclusion that this 40 percent rise in wages in the period from 1860 to 1891, which Bowley assumes to hold true for the entire working class of England, does not even hold true for all the strata of the labor aristocracy. Kautsky contends that the author simply *assumes* that the average general condition of the working class improved to the same extent as the condition of the workers organized in the trade unions; the latter however, do not constitute more than a fifth of all the workers. Kautsky proves that Bowley's figures are greatly exaggerated, that even the wages of the excellently organized workers in the British iron industry rose only by 25 percent in the period of time mentioned.

That is undoubtedly what really happened. The great mass of the unskilled workers led a lamentable existence. But the minority of the aristocrats of labor were bribed with small crumbs. Thus the bourgeoisie beheaded the movement of the British proletariat, so to speak. In England *organized* workers and skilled workers for a long time were synonymous. In the epoch of the old trade unionism the better-situated skilled workers constituted the main mass of the trade union membership. But even in the epoch of the new trade unionism this state of affairs has remained the same by and large.[30] The British trade unions still do not embrace more than a fifth of all the workers today. Many millions of women workers and of the most poorly paid unskilled workers are still unorganized, still outside the trade unions.

In 1902 Kautsky wrote, in characterizing the "upper strata of the British working class" (i.e., the labor aristocracy), that "today indeed they are scarcely more than little bourgeois and are distinguished from them only by a somewhat greater lack of culture. Their highest ideal consists in aping their masters and in maintaining their hypocritical respectability, their admiration for wealth, however it may be obtained, and their spiritless manner of killing their leisure time. The emancipation of their class appears to them as a foolish dream. Consequently, it is foot-ball, boxing, horse racing, and opportunities for gambling which move them the deepest and to which their entire leisure time, their individual powers, and their material means are devoted." (*The Social Revolution*, Chicago: Charles H. Kerr and Co., 1902, pp. 101–2.)

These "little bourgeois"—the labor aristocracy—served the big bourgeoisie as the best means of introducing bourgeois ideas into the laboring mass. By throwing down to these "little bourgeois" a few crumbs from their richly decked imperialist table, the big bourgeoisie made of them faithful watch-dogs of the capitalist system. With the aid of a thin golden thread it bound them firmly to the bandwagon of imperialism, made them into *agents of the bourgeoisie*, destined to demoralize systematically the labor movement and to inculcate it with the virus of opportunism. The "little bourgeois" became the most reliable advance guards of the imperialist bourgeoisie in the camp of the working class.

WHEN KAUTSKY SPEAKS of the bourgeois "respectability" of these "little bourgeois," he is only continuing in the tradition of Marx and Engels. Both of the founders of scientific socialism, who lived in England for a long time and therefore had the opportunity of acquainting themselves at first hand with the reactionary role of the labor aristocrats, advised their disciples continually to make just such an evaluation of the "little bourgeois" as we have found in Kautsky's passage above.

The most repugnant thing here (in England—G.Z.) is the bourgeois 'respectability', which has grown deep into the bones of the workers! The division of society into innumerable strata, each recognised without question, each with its own pride but also its inborn respect for its 'betters' and 'superiors', is so old and firmly established that the bourgeois still find it fairly easy to get their bait accepted. I am not at all sure, for instance, that John Burns is not secretly prouder of his popularity with Cardinal Manning, the Lord Mayor, and the bourgeoisie in general than of his popularity with his own class. And Champion—an ex-lieutenant—has always intrigued with bourgeois and especially conservative elements, preaching socialism at the parsons' Church Congress, etc. And even Tom Mann, whom I regard as the best of the lot, is fond of mentioning that he will be lunching with the Lord Mayor. [Karl Marx and Frederick Engels, *Selected Correspondence* (Moscow: Progress Publishers, 1975), p. 386.]

This is what Frederick Engels wrote as far back as 1889.

Even earlier, in 1882, Engels wrote in a letter to Kautsky, which is devoted especially to the question of the attitude of the British workers toward colonial policy, as follows: "You ask me what the English workers think about colonial policy. Well, exactly the same as they think about politics in general: the same as the bourgeoisie think. There is no workers party here, there are only Conservatives and Liberal-Radicals, and the workers are cheerfully consuming their share of England's monopoly of the world market and the colonies." [Marx and Engels, *Selected Correspondence,* pp. 330–31.]

Here we see a direct indication of the fact that the bourgeoisie *bribes* the workers by leaving them little tidbits from among the multitude of benefits which the British monopoly on the world market and in the colonies nets them.

In 1877 Marx speaks of the "shameful trade union congress at Leicester . . . where the bourgeois played the patron saints, among them a certain Mr. Th. Brassey, a multimillionaire . . . and the son of the notorious Brassey of the railroads, whose 'enterprise' is Europe and Asia." (*Briefe an Sorge,* p. 156.)

IN 1893 ENGELS upbraids the "socialist" Fabians in the following words:

> The Fabians are a gang of careerists here in London who have understanding enough to realise the inevitability of the social revolution, but who could not possibly entrust this gigantic task to the raw proletariat alone and are therefore kind enough to put themselves at the head. Fear of the revolution is their fundamental principle. . . . Hence their tactics of not resolutely fighting the Liberals as adversaries but of pushing them on towards Socialist conclusions and therefore of intriguing with them, of permeating Liberalism with Socialism. . . . These people have of course many bourgeois followers and therefore money. . . .
>
> It is a critical moment for the movement here. . . . There was a moment when it nearly came under the wing of Champion—who consciously or unconsciously works just as much for the

Tories as the Fabians do for the Liberals. . . . But
. . . socialism has penetrated the masses in the
industrial districts enormously in the last few years
and I am counting on these masses to keep the
leaders in hand. [Marx and Engels, *On Britain*
(Moscow: Foreign Languages Publishing House,
1953), pp. 532–33.]

These were the views of Marx and Engels on the "little bourgeois," the labor aristocracy. They stigmatized the antirevolutionary position of these strata unsparingly, whether it expressed itself in the policies of trade unionism or in the socialist organization of the Fabians. From every word uttered by Marx and Engels on this question, it is clearly evident how fatal for the cause of the workers, how disastrous for the socialist struggle of the proletariat, they considered the specific point of view of the labor aristocracy.

Marx and Engels derived their generalizations regarding the role of the labor bureaucracy mainly from their observations of the process of development of the working class in England. It was in England, moreover, that Marx made his studies of capitalism in general. In his *Capital*, also, Marx cites above all else, from the experiences of British capitalism. But a great deal of water has passed under the bridge since then. The conservative role of the labor aristocracy may be observed today, not only in England, but in a large number of other countries.

Let us take Holland, for example. Here is a small country that does not dream today of dominating the world market. But in this country there is a bourgeoisie bursting with wealth, whose few remnants of past colonial grandeur still bring it annually a golden shower of irrationally big profits. Of these unheard-of profits of the Dutch imperialist bourgeoisie, only the "upper" strata of the workers enjoy a crumb or two, but that suffices to constitute them into a labor aristocracy, which becomes, in turn, a conservative, counterrevolutionary element.

A<small>ND IN AMERICA</small>? Do we not witness the spectacle there of a tiny group of labor aristocrats rising on the backs of a millions-strong mass of oppressed workers—particularly of immigrants and Negroes—and bought out and nurtured by the financial oligarchy? Are not Gompers and Company agents of the bourgeoisie in the circles of the "aristocrats of labor," and are not the latter, in turn, agents of Gompers in the camp of the working class? On the one hand, workers are shot down in the course of purely economic strikes; on the other, Gompers and the other "stainless knights of labor" are decorated with ever greater honors, almost with titular decorations.

Or in Australia. The social-liberals treasure Australia as the Promised Land, in which a coal miner can become a minister. But what has actually happened? Here too, a small parasitic band of labor leaders—the Messrs. Fisher, Hughes, and Company[31]—rise upon the shoulders of the oppressed mass of unskilled workers and, brought to the surface by a little group of labor aristocrats, are betraying the interests of the working class with a cynicism unprecedented in history. The crisis created by the outbreak of the World War has thrown a particularly strong light upon this despicable treachery of the "labor leaders."

This self-same sort of bribery took place among the "upper strata" of the workers in Germany as well. Under different conditions, in a somewhat different form, it ran its course in the land of the "classic social democracy." But the historical sense of the transformation undergone by the heads of the German working class, in the persons of the leaders of their trade unions and of their so-called social democratic party, is not the same. There is no serious difference between Legien, Gompers, Fisher, and Henderson. Legien is not a minister as yet, but for reasons entirely independent of his own person. In the period immediately ahead of us he may not get any further than the ministerial antechamber. The Prussian Junkers will continue to extend only one finger at a time to him. But he is, nevertheless, only a "labor lieutenant of the capitalist class." And not only Legien, but naturally also Scheidemann and Südekum, as well as all their carbon copies, whose manner of speech, alone, differs from the former's. The process of the transition of the German labor aristocracy to the side of the bourgeoisie naturally did not begin yesterday. The corruption of the labor aristocracy began with the entrance of German imperialism into the world arena. The more far-sighted of the ideologists of the German bourgeoisie have given (and still give) an excellent account of this social phenomenon, so all-important for the bourgeoisie. Professor Schmoller tells us that the German bourgeoisie had made peaceful overtures to the "patriotic labor movement" as far back as the beginning of the nineties. The social democracy, he says, did not, however, take the extended hand at once. "Only a wise politician like Herr von Vollmar was ready at that time to make the turn and thus to lend an impulse to revisionism."

It was not the social democrats alone who did not want to make peace, however. The extremists among the ruling classes, the Junkers, the bitterest reactionaries, also resisted. They saw in the German social democracy a revolutionary danger and relied more and more on exterminating it by means of reprisals. The voices of the more sensible bourgeois were drowned out by the howls of the reactionaries. "The voices of the nonpartisans, who . . . denied . . . the alleged danger of revolution . . . were not given a hearing." Professor Schmoller today complains against the irreconcilables.

In any case, the conflict inside of the ruling classes has now been settled. There isn't a single Purishkevitch in Germany today who doesn't understand that it is necessary to make certain "concessions" to well-meaning workers.[32] The danger of revolution has proved to be an "alleged" danger. The system of "bribery" has withstood the test brilliantly.

Speaking in retrospect, the well-known bourgeois professor, Dr. Herkner, the author of *Labor Problems,* writes: "Only in the course of the last ten to fifteen years, views have gradually come forward, in the columns of the revisionist *Sozialistische Monatshefte,* to be precise, which herald a distinct return to more forceful nationalistic political ideas. . . . Considerable strata of labor have achieved such a remarkable improvement in their social conditions and have found the advantages accruing also to them—due to the powerful boom in German economic life—of such immediate promise, that they themselves have displayed a most intense interest in this boom. The old slogans of internationalism, such as that the workers had no fatherland or that they had nothing to lose but their chains, are no longer taken seriously by even the most rabid of the comrades."

However, this question has been dealt with in similar fashion by the most influential representatives of German imperialism, not only at the present time, after 1914, but long before the war. In the very scholarly work of the prominent German conservative, Baron von Waltershausen, devoted to the question of capital exports, a number of pages deal especially with the problem of the extent to which workers are "interested" in the imperialism of their country. "Both capital and labor are equally concerned about territorial and maritime defenses," writes this erudite baron. "The laboring population is, moreover, participating directly in the dividends derived. Insofar as that serves for the consumption of those benefiting therefrom, it brings about a substantial demand for goods and services on the internal market and thus helps raise the wages of workers and servants. If the dividends accrue to the domestic enterprises in the form of a greater accumulation of capital, then the latter also experience the need to employ more labor power." These few words—and though the expressions used are rather unusual—contain the entire theory of social chauvinism.

REGARDING THE SITUATION in England, Sartorius von Waltershausen writes as follows: "The immense national wealth accumulated in England in the course of the last century has become—although industry itself has retrogressed—a protection for the class of skilled workers." And he quotes Schulze-Gaevernitz approvingly: "The skilled and well-paid work force of British heavy industry has realized today that the high standard of living it has achieved with such difficulty, stands and falls with England's political power."

This is plain talk. The British imperialists bribe a part of their labor aristocracy. We, the German imperialists, must also learn to buy out "our" labor aristocracy. The learned representative of German junkerdom sees very clearly the connection between "labor" opportunism and "labor" imperialism, between imperialist victories and the transition of the labor aristocracy to the side of the bourgeoisie. Regarding England, he maintains that no social democracy could arise there as long as the British imperialists had the means of bribing their workers. The example of Germany proves, however, that this is not entirely correct: a social democracy *can* exist also under such conditions; not a revolutionary, but rather a counterrevolutionary social democracy a la Südekum. There is one more thing that Mr. Sartorius von Waltershausen has forgotten; namely, that a genuine social democracy aims to be not the party of the labor aristocracy, but rather the party of the *working class* as a whole. He has overlooked the fact that the skilled and better-paid workers form only a minority of the working class—a minority which, when it goes over to the side of the imperialists at the critical moment, can deal the socialist movement quite a blow, to be sure, but never uproot it.

We have already said that the entire theory of modern social chauvinism is contained essentially in the quoted passages from Waltershausen and Schmoller. The "theoreticians" of social chauvinism today draw almost exclusively from this imperialist source. "Truths" such as those propagated by imperialists like Waltershausen for years are recast by them somewhat and painted over with a Marxist veneer to serve for use among the workers. What the Messrs. social chauvinists dish up for the masses as socialism today is in reality little more than the perfected theory of the community of interests between the imperialist bourgeoisie and the "little bourgeoisie," the labor aristocrats.

What indeed, is the basic thesis of Cunow, Legien, Winnig, Lensch, Scheidemann, and their consorts?[33] We, they say, support "our" government and "our" bourgeoisie, not at all because we like its looks. No, the interests of the German *working class* demand an ever stronger development of "our" fatherland's capitalism, demand that the economic progress of our country proceed as rapidly and as freely as possible, that "we" find a sufficiently great number of export markets, or sources of raw materials, of spheres of influence of "our" capital, etc. Only then will the demand for labor power be big enough, only then will the living standard of the workers rise. When our capitalists make more profits there will be something left over for the workers as well.

But the same picture unfolds before us on the opposite side. It is not only "we" alone that are interested in the profits of "our" bourgeoisie; the workers of other countries that compete with "us" have identical interests in relation to "their" bourgeoisie. When the contest for colonies, for the "freedom of the seas," has been sharpened to its highest pitch, war breaks out. What is to be done? It is a tragic necessity. The workers would naturally prefer to settle such matters peacefully, but that is not always possible. War has become a fact. What shall the German workers do? Shall they refuse to support their government and their bourgeoisie? But in that case, Germany will suffer defeat. And that will mean that the development of capitalism in Germany will be retarded, that the demand for labor power will decline, that the German workers will be forced to emigrate in order to earn their bread on foreign shores, to content themselves with low wages. What else can the German workers do if they are to avoid this misfortune? Only one thing: support "their" government, "their" imperialism. We know—Legien, Lensch, and Winnig say—that imperialism has its bad features, that it is bound up with wars, etc. But these are far outweighed by its good features. Thanks to imperialism the living standard of our working class has been rising. We know, say these leaders of the official German social democracy, that when we support our imperialism, we thereby take up arms against the workers of other countries. That is truly very sad—but we have no choice in the matter. A tragic necessity remains a necessity nevertheless.

And what does this tragic necessity really prove? Only that in practice, in living reality, the actual interests of the workers of the various countries do not at all coincide. Often the interests of the workers in one country stand in an irreconcilable conflict with the interests of the workers of another country. "Workers of all countries, unite!" That sounds very good, but what can be done if the economic interests, practically speaking, do not unite the proletarians of the various countries, but rather divide them?

Lensch writes:

> We are thus in a position to recognize also the historic causes which led to the collapse of the International. *Theoretically the solidarity of interests among the proletariat of the great industrial countries did exist to be sure, but not yet practically.* . . . International solidarity of the proletariat was valid only as a slogan in the social democracy. But this solidarity—and this is one of the great new realizations brought home to us by the war—is by no means to be determined in advance. . . . It presupposes a certain equality of status among the powers involved. As long as one nation is so superior to another as to be regarded as a world dominion, this contrast, insofar as it is a matter of the other nations standing in opposition to a single world

dominion, is transposed upon their respective working classes as well. The war opened the eyes of the German social democracy to this fact: that, historically considered, it is still too early to speak of an international solidarity of the working class.

The standpoint of consistent social chauvinism is so clearly formulated here as to leave nothing more to be desired in the way of clarity. International solidarity is a great ideal. But in practice the economic interests of the working classes in the individual countries "still" require their solidarity with "their" bourgeoisie, with "their" imperialism.

It is necessary to investigate only one small matter yet: *Is it true,* as the social chauvinists contend, that the whole working class benefits from a boom on the part of its domestic imperialism, that its economic living standard actually rises and that its wages are raised? Or have not Legien, Lensch (as well as their imitators) perhaps *confused the working class with the labor aristocracy?* And, in the case of the latter, have they not also confused a transitory material advantage with much more profound and more permanent interests?

BUT FIRST, another question: Have Marxists dealt with these problems *before* the war and what answer did they give then? When we ask ourselves this question, we must say: *yes,* of course these problems were dealt with before the war; it was impossible to avoid them because all these "proofs" of the social chauvinists for the necessity of supporting imperialism were at that time zealously propagated by the *bourgeoisie* itself, because the politicians and ideologists of imperialism disseminated them far and wide. And what must now be directed as a reply to the Lensches of all countries was cited back at that time in the polemics against the Waltershausens of all languages. Let us, for example, hear what Otto Bauer has to say on the subject[34]—we purposely refrain from quoting theoreticians belonging to the Marxist left wing; we pick, instead, a representative of the moderate "Marxist center."

> The struggle for export markets serves this same purpose, just as in the case of the struggle for spheres of influence. The decrease in fixed capital, the speeding up of its circulation into the sphere of production, the extension of the period of production inside of the period of the turnover as a whole, all these appear to be the common interests of all the classes. The working class also appears to have a stake in this process: if the mass of monetary capital withdrawn from capital circulation at a given moment is decreased, the demand for labor power grows, the position of the worker on the labor market is strengthened, wages are raised. It is therefore taken for granted that the worker's interest as a producer favors protective tariffs and expansion policy. (Otto Bauer: *Die Nationalitätenfrage und die Sozialdemokratie* [The National Question and the Social Democracy], *Marxstudien*, vol. 2.)

Otto Bauer analyzes thoroughly this whole chain of syllogisms characteristic of bourgeois political economy (we know that all these "socialist" officials have made this bourgeois political economy their own) and reaches the following conclusion:

Bourgeois economics has observed that modern tariff policy and colonial policy changes the *circulation* of capital and that these changes emphasize the tendency toward a rise in prices, profits, and wages. That is why capitalist expansion policy appears, from that point of view, to be just as advantageous to the interests of the workers as it is to the interests of the capitalist class.

But that is *not* so, says Bauer, adding:

> Protective tariffs force society to produce those commodities for which the conditions of production are less favorable in a particular country. Thus the tariff reduces the productivity of social labor. This is evident from the high prices of the commodities thus produced. In this way the purchasing power of money is reduced and the working class suffers harm. . . . Higher commodity prices, a decreased purchasing power of money with wages remaining stationary, these are the first effects of capitalist tariff policy insofar as the working class is concerned.
> If we compare the distribution of productive capital under the influence of the protective tariff with the distribution of productive capital under the conditions of free trade, we find a far greater share of social capital flowing into branches of production which, capital investments remaining equal, employ less labor power than the other industries. The protective tariff, therefore, reduces the demand for labor power and deteriorates the position of the worker on the labor market. More than that! The industries favored by the trust-protecting tariff are such in which capital

has reached the highest point of concentration, in which the mobility of the workers has been almost abolished and the trade union struggle extraordinarily impeded. . . . By favoring the heavy industries, by damaging the industries using iron and steel as raw materials, the protective tariff transposes capital into branches of production that offer the least advantageous conditions for the struggle of the trade unions.

Furthermore, imperialism requires immense military resources. Tremendous sums must be sacrificed for military and naval purposes. The sober observer will only be able to justify imperialist policies if the economic advantages resulting from them outweigh these economic sacrifices. This question also is posed differently for the working class than it is for the bourgeoisie. *For everywhere a far greater part of labor's wages than of surplus value is sacrificed to militarism.* . . . The capitalist states . . . are determined to impose the costs of military armaments upon the working class. Thus the decline in the rate of accumulation is prevented, for a far smaller part is accumulated from labor's wages than from surplus value. When the worker has to surrender a considerable part of his wages as taxes to the state, then the individual consumption of the worker is reduced in favor of state consumption in the form of expenditures for militarism. . . . The concern over the level of the rate of accumulation alone instigates all capitalist states . . . to balance the budget for the army and the navy by means of indirect taxes and revenues which burden the working class far more heavily than the owning classes.

Capital exports effect a sinking demand on

the European labor market. ... A decrease in the nation's desire for work signifies in capitalist society a decline in the demand for its labor forces, a deterioration of the condition of the workers on the labor market. Insofar as imperialism favors the emigration of European capital to foreign parts of the globe, it threatens altogether too directly the workers' "interests as producers." By extending the arena for the leveling of the rate of profit to the entire face of the earth, imperialism aims at the displacement of European labor by the cheaper labor of the less advanced nations, which therefore signifies—as Kurt Eisner once said[35]—a tendency toward a general lockout of the European working class. ... Does not the exploitation of the most impoverished and most despised worker in the entire world, the Chinese coolie—directly detrimental as it is to the cause of the workers in all countries—indeed furnish us with a remarkable example of the international solidarity of the workers' interests?

Imperialism thus decreases the share of the working class in social wealth, transforms the relationship between the amount of values accruing to the possessing classes and those appropriated by the working class to the detriment of the proletariat, thus increasing the *exploitation* of the workers.

This is the conclusion Otto Bauer reaches. Schippel's views,[36] shared today by the whole social chauvinist cult from Lensch to Maslow, are characterized by Bauer as bourgeois views. Schippel is carrying on *"not proletarian, but capitalist, not social democratic, but national-liberal policies."*

It is of no use to the proletariat in an economic sense; that is quite beyond questioning. However, "(imperialism) furnishes the ruling classes with ever greater masses of armed men serving as their involuntary instruments. Thereby it becomes a danger to democracy. . . . The working-class youth form the backbone of the modern (conscript people's) armies. How can workers overlook the question whether an increase of profits is really of such an invaluable benefit that it must be paid for with the lives of thousands upon thousands (today we must add millions—G.Z.) of hopeful young men?"

A<small>LL THIS WAS A SELF-EVIDENT TRUTH</small> recognized by all adherents to the labor movement before the war, by all—save that little band of gentlemen who even at that time openly served the bourgeoisie, like Schippel and Company. And now? What can the Messrs. social chauvinists reply to the proofs furnished by Otto Bauer? Absolutely nothing! They do not even attempt to refute these proofs, which were once flung in the face of the bourgeoisie, but which today apply so perfectly to the official "theory" of the modern also-socialists.

There can be no question that imperialism does not result in any advantages whatsoever for *the working class as a whole*. But it cannot be denied that for a *certain minority* of skilled workers, for the *labor aristocracy*, a few crumbs may fall off from the imperialist table. Bauer came quite close to such a conclusion when he wrote: "Certainly the protective tariff has the effect of channeling a greater share of capital into branches of production with a highly organic composition—that is, with a far lower capacity for the absorption of labor forces than that which would ordinarily have found a place for itself in these branches of industry. The branches of production which require a great deal of constant, but very little variable, capital (i.e., few workers—G.Z.) are most mature for trustification. The export practices of these trusts, based upon the protective tariffs, aim to *strike* at similar branches of production abroad with a low organic composition" (i.e., a relatively greater number of workers.—G.Z.).

A SMALL MINORITY of skilled workers, those employed by the branches of industry enumerated by Bauer (and in several others), actually do feed on imperialism. But it is a *dwindling minority* of the working class. The experience of the World War has proved this in particularly striking fashion. The condition of the great mass of workers has—due to the frightfully high cost of living and the suspension of the protective labor laws, etc.—become considerably more *miserable*. Millions of women and children working at starvation wages have been drawn into the process of production. The economic situation of the entire great mass of, let us say, the British workers, has undergone an absolute deterioration. Only a small minority—some two million workers—have succeeded in retaining their former real wages (i.e., an increase in wages corresponding to the rise in the prices of the necessities most in demand); only in the rarest cases are present-day wages higher than those of prewar days.

Yet there can be no doubt as to the existence of a small layer of labor aristocrats whom the cannon and munition kings do throw a bone occasionally from their rich feast of war profits. This minority made good wages even before the war and has enjoyed still higher wages during the war. All kinds of privileges were granted this minority before the war, also. During the course of the war these privileges have become far more valuable for these aristocrats of labor. It is sufficient to point out that this labor aristocracy *has not been sent to the front* in most cases. The industrialists need them at home; they are indispensable as the element under whose direction the ordinary workers, the women, the youth, and the children are carrying on their work in the factories and in the mills and mines.

It is these very narrow, group interests of this minority of privileged labor aristocrats that the social chauvinists have confused with the interests of the working class. This confusion is quite understandable when we grasp the fact that the leaders of the trade unions and of the official social democracy hail, in their majority, from that very same environment of the labor aristocracy. The labor aristocracy and the labor bureaucracy are two blood brothers. When the social chauvinists speak of the interests of the working class, they have in mind—often quite unconsciously—the interests of the labor aristocracy. But here too, it is not really a matter of veritable interests in the broader meaning of the word, so much as of immediate material advantages. This is absolutely not one and the same thing. Marxists have never held the view that the realization of the interests of the workers means to fill their pockets as much as possible. From the point of view of interests, understood in the more profound sense of the term, the labor aristocracy is committing *treason against itself.* For, the "aristocrats of labor" remain wage slaves for all that. Temporarily they do enjoy a certain advantage, to be sure, but they thereby undermine their own position and violate the unity of the working class. They sell their birthright for a mess of pottage. They retard the erection of a new order in society which will of necessity free them, the "aristocrats" themselves, from wage slavery. They become a tool of reaction.

Look at the bourgeoisie. We are inclined to believe that its basic principle is the immediate interest in the fate of its pocketbook. But the bourgeoisie understands only too well that it must subordinate this "principle" to its *general* class interests. It would be easy to prove to the bourgeoisie that a people's militia is considerably less expensive than a standing army, that it is much more preferable from the point of view of immediate interests. But the bourgeoisie will nevertheless prefer, as a rule, the much more expensive standing army. And in doing so, its point of departure will always be the more important *class interest* of the bourgeoisie.

To foster splits between the various strata of the working class, to promote competition among them, to segregate the upper stratum from the rest by corrupting it and by making it an agency for bourgeois "respectability"—that is entirely in the interests of the bourgeoisie. Even if we were to disregard the *political* interests of the working class, the social chauvinists would still be traitors to the cause of the workers. For even in the field of protecting the *economic* interests they cannot see further than their noses. They identify economic interests with a temporary advantage amounting to a few more pennies. They split the working class inside of every country and thereby intensify and aggravate the split between the working classes of the various countries. Thanks to the common efforts of the bourgeoisie and the social chauvinists, the world proletariat is being split horizontally as well as vertically, if we may be permitted to use these terms.

We have said that the official "European" labor organizations—particularly its leading strata—are recruited in the main from the better-paid workers. From the labor aristocracy. Is that correct? Are there sufficient objective and well-founded proofs to substantiate this contention? These proofs are, beyond a doubt, at hand.

Let us turn once more to the *German* labor movement as the classic example of a labor movement in this past epoch. The composition of the German Social Democratic Party and of the German trade unions is certainly more proletarian in character than that of any other "European" party. And what do we see? The German social democracy has not provided for extensive statistics regarding the social composition of its whole party organization. But such statistics do exist and may, to a certain extent, be regarded as symptomatic for the entire party.

W<small>E HAVE BEFORE US</small> an excellent piece of statistical research regarding the composition of the Berlin social democratic organization; it was compiled some eight or nine years ago, but may still be considered as quite valid even today.

Berlin is the largest labor center and the strongest pillar of German social democracy. The data relates to the years 1906 and 1907; they encompass some 53,106 organized workers, members of the Social Democratic Party (81 percent of all the members organized into the Social Democratic Party in Berlin at that time). At first glance two circumstances command our attention in this extremely interesting piece of statistical research. First, the existence of a numerically strong group of nonworkers in the social democratic organization, who are designated as "independents." Second, the relatively *poor* percentage of party members recruited from the mass of unskilled workers. The group of "independents," that is, people who do *not* live by the sale of their labor power, consists of some 5,228 men (out of 53,106), i.e., amounts to 9.8 percent of all the party members under investigation. Nearly 10 percent of all the organized Social Democrats in the city of Berlin and its environs are, therefore, not workers. Of the 5,228 "independents," nearly half are innkeepers. They are 2,528 men strong in this group. Then there are 452 independent barbers, 310 merchants and shopkeepers, and 74 factory owners. The other "independents" are recruited from among owners of printshops and artisans, commission agents, artists, etc. Thus, at least one out of every ten members of the Berlin organization of the social democracy belongs to the petty bourgeoisie. The owners of inns, barbershops, etc., are in most cases intimately linked with the working-class population. Workers are the chief customers of this sort of commercial enterprise. Nevertheless, the interests of the workers and the interests of these groups often diverge.

Undoubtedly a distinct petty-bourgeois current is introduced into the Social Democratic Party by this stratum of so-called independents. Thousands of innkeepers, hundreds of small manufacturers, merchants, and independent tradesmen—these are not individuals who have adopted the point of view of the proletariat. This is an entire, distinct stratum which has retained its own interests, its own psychology, its own mode of thinking.

On the other hand, we find the following things worthy of note in these Berlin statistics: The authors of the work have segregated the unskilled workers into a separate category under the classification of "workers"—without any further supplementary description. And what is the result? The unskilled workers amounted to 14.9 percent, all told, of the entire number of members of the Berlin social democratic organization under investigation. In the First Electoral District of Berlin they amounted to 2.5 percent of all the organized; in the Third District, to 5.6

percent; in the Fifth, to 7.9 percent. Thus it follows that the predominant mass of the membership of the Berlin social democratic organization is composed of *trained,* of *skilled workers.* In other words, *the predominant mass of the membership of the social democratic organization consists of the better-paid strata of labor—of those strata from which the greatest section of the labor aristocracy arises.*

THIS CONCLUSION is also confirmed by the statistics regarding the trade unions, which are particularly thoroughgoing in the research work we have mentioned. What branches show the highest percentage in trade union organization? Among the compositors and pressmen, 90.6 percent are organized (of the 10,986 printers employed in Berlin, 9,850 are members of the free trade unions). Among the lithographers, 90.5 percent are organized; among the engravers, 75.6 percent; among the metalworkers, 68.7 percent. In the textile industry, on the other hand, the organized workers are only 21.4 percent of the total. Of the garment workers, only 10 percent are organized; of the transport workers, only 25.3 percent; of the tobacco workers, 34.3 percent; of the bakers, 34.1 percent; of the shoeworkers, 34.7 percent. The picture is the same throughout. No matter how big the membership of the free trade unions may be (before the outbreak of the war they comprised over 3 million organized workers)—they do *not* include in their ranks the great mass of the unskilled workers. The free trade unions have succeeded in organizing only a small minority (one-fifth) of the workers. The predominant mass of their workers are likewise recruited from among the skilled, the better-paid, category of workers.

Returning once more to the statistics covering the

membership of the Social Democratic Party of Greater Berlin, we can draw the following balance sheet: The great mass of the unskilled workers, of the most exploited and most oppressed section of the proletariat, is very feebly represented in the German Social Democratic Party. It constitutes within it a group of no more than 15 percent in strength, at best. On the opposite pole to this group we have a numerically almost as strong (10 percent) group of nonworkers, namely, innkeepers, barbers, merchants, etc. This group may be smaller in number than that of the unskilled workers. But its influence on party affairs—that may be said a priori—is incomparably bigger. The "independent" elements are far more mobile; far less preoccupied with physical labor; dispose of a far greater amount of free time; are in a position to offer the party material services; their social position is on a much higher plane; they are the ones that are put up as the party's candidates in the elections, etc. *Between* these two groups, which represent opposite poles, stand the better situated, more skilled workers, the real props of the Social Democratic Party organization. The main body, the central organism of the party, is thus formed of these strata of *skilled* workers.

IN THE PREVIOUS SECTION we have acquainted ourselves with the social composition of the electorate of the German social democracy and discovered the existence of a large group of petty bourgeois among it. The same symptoms—even though of a different numerical relationship, perhaps—can be established in the composition of the party organization as well.

Among the petty-bourgeois elements of the German Social Democratic Party organization, the innkeepers, particularly, play an important role. We have already seen how strongly they are represented in the Berlin party organization. In the province of Leipzig the number of "organized" social democratic innkeepers amounted to 87 (1.7 percent of all members of the local organization) in 1900; in the city of Leipzig, to 63 (3.4 percent of all the members) in 1905; in Offenbach, to 76 (4.6 percent) in 1905; in Munich, to 39 (5.5 percent); in Frankfurt on the Main, to 25 (1 percent); in Reinickendorf (near Berlin), to 18 (5.9 percent). According to Michels's figures, there is, in the various localities, one "social democratic" innkeeper to every twenty party members. In the social democratic Reichstag fraction there were four innkeepers (out of 35 deputies) in 1892; five innkeepers (out of 58) in 1903; six (out of 81) in 1905. In Berlin there has been organized a special—and very strong—association of social democratic innkeepers. Workers constitute the greatest bulk of their customers and that draws the owners of inns and restaurants much closer to the workers. On the other hand, the workers need meeting halls. The cheaper restaurants in the working-class neighborhoods, the inns, therefore, serve the organized workers as hangouts and as meeting places. According to their economic position, however, many innkeepers are much closer in their relationship to the petty and middle bourgeoisie than they are to the proletariat. Often they themselves exploit the wage workers. Often their interests are opposed to the interests of the organized workers, and hostile clashes occur between them—as, for example, in the case of workers boycotting breweries or when workers carry on antialcoholic propaganda.

The influence of this whole group of members of the Social Democratic Party is often quite substantial. Particularly in the smaller cities, a good deal of the social democratic organization, if not all of it, depends upon them. Professor Schmoller contends that anywhere from one-third to one-half of the entire Social Democratic Party are not workers at all. That they are radical petty bourgeois. That the party has therefore tended to become more and more of a radical-democratic coalition party. Insofar as the quantitative side of the whole matter is concerned, Professor Schmoller may be painting things a bit too thick. But in relation to its qualitative side, his evaluation is correct. The official German social democracy has actually become more and more of a radical-democratic coalition party. That is just what the opportunists wanted and they have led the party on this path with full consciousness. Bernstein was right in one respect, when he said at the beginning of his campaign against Marxism: We need not fear to call things by their right names—to say that we are simply a party of democratic reforms.

THE PETTY-BOURGEOIS ELEMENTS have laid their stakes in the ranks of the official social democracy—they constitute one of the sources of opportunism. The labor aristocracy—that is the second source, the second channel, through which the contagion of opportunism penetrated the party. Often one is struck point blank by this very insistence of the labor aristocracy on taking the path of opportunism. Take the printers, for example. It is noteworthy that in Germany—as well as in France, Italy, Holland, Switzerland, etc.—the typographical unions stand far more to the right than the general run of the already quite conservative trade union movements of these different countries. In Germany, the opportunist Rexhauser heads the printing crafts; in France it is the opportunist

Keufer. In Belgium and Holland the workers engaged in the diamond-cutting industry form the bulwark of opportunism. And these are not isolated examples.

The bourgeois opponents of socialism know that only too well. "The more the worker gains in importance, the more realistic he is inclined to be; he places his laurel wreath on the unforgettable head of Karl Marx in its fine marble cast and pays higher dues into the trade union treasury," writes Pastor Naumann, not without a touch of irony, in his article entitled "The Fortunes of Marxism."[37] In the same article this Naumann, one of the ideological leaders of German imperialism, writes: "The words, 'Proletarians of all countries, unite!' have had their effect. We are now faced with numbers of organized people whom no one had previously given a thought. There is money in the treasuries—as much as one could want. . . . Are there still not enough organized? Why is everything so quiet all around us? Where is the even step of those brass boots?"

Maximilian Harden, Ludwig Stelin, Werner Sombart, and the others mock at the German social democracy in a much similar vein.[38] In the course of its development the German social democracy is losing more and more of its revolutionary "venom." Its need for peace and for order is becoming constantly greater. It is becoming a *conservative* party.

The more far-sighted bourgeois have long ago noted this process. They know "their" social democracy only too well. One of the social-liberal German professors, Max Weber,[39] a colleague of Sombart's, once turned with this counsel to the German princes: If you want to be radically cured of your fright from social democracy, you should attend one of the Social Democratic Party conventions. He advised them to look over the delegates at these conventions from the spectators' gallery and become convinced that among these revolutionaries, among these overthrowers of the state, it is the physiognomies of good-natured innkeepers and typical petty bourgeois that predominate. They would soon become convinced that there is not a trace of revolutionary enthusiasm among them.

Unfortunately, the social-liberal professor was right. The crisis of the World War has proved that the official German social democracy is not only not revolutionary, but directly counterrevolutionary. Only in *opposition* to this official social democracy, only in the struggle against the specific "interests" of the labor aristocracy, can the road be paved for a truly socialist movement in Germany, as well as in the other countries.

NOTES

1. On August 4, 1914, immediately on the outbreak of the first World War, the German Social Democratic Party rallied to the support of German imperialism by voting for the financial estimates ("war credits") for the war effort. The Socialist Party in France and the Labour Party in Britain did the same, joining coalition governments to prosecute the war. Leaders of the Social Democratic Party in Austria-Hungary also backed "their" government in the war. Although in Italy and some other countries the majority of socialists did not fall in step with this outright chauvinism, only in Russia, among the great powers, did a major socialist party hold true to the revolutionary principles of Marxism. Here the Bolshevik Party led by V.I. Lenin not only opposed the tsarist regime's war effort, but also utilized the growing war crisis to press toward socialist revolution.

August 4 represented the collapse of the Second (or Socialist) International, an international association of socialist parties founded in 1889. Its official bodies no longer functioned and its leaders no longer met. The Bolsheviks led its left-wing minority in preparing the ground for a new, genuinely working-class International.

"Opportunism" designates the class-collaborationist right wing of the socialist parties, which had gained strength before 1914. The opportunists, also called "revisionists," sought to direct all the party's energies toward achieving whatever modest reforms seemed possible within the existing capitalist system and existing relationship of class forces, projecting a gradual and peaceful evolution to socialism in this way.

"Chauvinism" refers to the racist and reactionary nationalism of an oppressor nation, of an imperialist ruling class. "Social chauvinism" refers to the chauvinism of those who purport to represent the working class.

When the ruling class unleashed war hysteria in August 1914, virtually all opportunists became social chauvinists, backing the imperialist war. So too did many who had previously been counted part of the Marxist left wing of the International.

2. Before 1914, all socialists were known as "social democrats," the name taken at the end of the nineteenth century by the German party, the largest and most influential in the International. After 1917 "social democracy" came to designate the opportunist and social chauvinist parties in the workers movement.

3. The year 1848 witnessed a European-wide revolutionary upsurge. In Germany, popular insurrections in Vienna and Berlin led to the formation of a National Assembly, based in Frankfurt. The main tasks of the bourgeois revolution in Germany were the elimination of the power of the feudal nobility, the establishment of democratic, constitutional rule, and the unification of the country. Alarmed at the scope of the struggle and the specter of the emerging German proletariat, however, the bourgeoisie sought to rein in the revolution and to make a compromise deal with the nobility. Marx and Engels

were active leaders in the revolution. They attacked this betrayal and concluded that the German bourgeoisie could no longer play a revolutionary role. Many of their conclusions are contained in Engels's book *Revolution and Counter-Revolution in Germany*. Most of Germany was ultimately unified with the foundation in 1871 of the German Empire, in which the feudal aristocrats continued to enjoy vast political and social privileges.

4. The Junkers were the landed aristocracy of Prussia. They retained a decisive grip on political power under the German Empire of 1871–1918.

5. These four individuals were leading figures in the Social Democratic Party's right wing. Wolfgang Heine (1861–?) was minister of the interior in Prussia after 1918; Albert Südekum (1871–?) was an extreme social chauvinist and a member of the Reichstag; Otto Landsberg (1869–?) became a member of the German provisional government in 1918; Eduard David (1863–1930), a Reichstag deputy from 1903, was an outspoken apologist for German imperialism.

6. In imperial Germany of 1871 to 1918, the Reichstag was the chamber of the federal parliament that was elected by universal male suffrage. It enjoyed only limited political power.

7. The Center was the party of the conservative Catholic hierarchy. The Conservatives represented above all the Junkers, the large landowners. The National Liberal Party traditionally spoke for German big business, which was still excluded by the landed aristocrats from direct political hegemony over the state.

8. The antisocialist laws were adopted in 1878 on the initiative of German Chancellor Otto von Bismarck. They banned all social democratic organizations and publications, allowing only parliamentary activity. During the following years of severe government repression, the socialists conducted vigorous underground activity and continued to expand their mass influence and electoral support. The laws were repealed in 1890.

9. Zinoviev is referring to the reply by August Bebel to a 1905 article by Dr. R. Blank on "The Social Composition of the Social Democratic Electorate in Germany." Bebel (1840–1913) was a founder of the German Social Democratic Party and its central leader for many years. He played a prominent role in the Second International. Toward the end of his life, he leaned toward centrist views on a number of questions and was severely criticized by Rosa Luxemburg and other left-wing Social Democrats.

10. The "Center" was the term used after 1910 to signify the group around Karl Kautsky (1854–1938) and the journal *Die Neue Zeit*. While portraying itself as orthodox Marxist and opposing revisionism verbally, this grouping increasingly adapted to the growing opportunist tendencies within the SDP, providing them with a left cover. When the First World War broke out, Kautsky and other centrists justified support for German imperialism on the grounds of "national defense." As mass opposition to the war grew among workers and found expression in strikes and large demonstrations, the centrists shifted to oppose the chauvinist policies of the SPD majority from a pacifist viewpoint; in 1916 they began to abstain or vote against the war credits. Still, they held to their stand of "national defense," sought to preserve unity with the proimperialist right wing, and to block moves to build a genuine workers party in Germany and a new workers' International. Although they left the SPD in 1917, they still joined with the SPD during the German revolution of 1918 to form a coalition government to preserve German capitalism.

11. Rosa Luxemburg (1871–1919) was a founder of the Polish Social Democratic Party and, after 1897, a leader of the revolutionary wing of the German socialist movement. An outstanding defender of and propagandist for Marxism, she sharply criticized Karl Kautsky's drift to the right in the years before 1914. Together with Karl Liebknecht, Luxemburg led the internationalist opposition in Germany to the First World War. Jailed in 1915, she helped found the Spartakusbund

(Spartacus League), Germany's most influential revolutionary current during the war. She was freed by the German revolution of November 1918, and helped found the German Communist Party. After the brutal crushing of the Berlin workers' uprising in January 1919, Luxemburg and Karl Liebknecht were arrested by order of the Social Democratic government. They were subsequently assassinated.

12. In the 1912 Reichstag elections, the German Social Democratic Party sought an alliance with two procapitalist liberal parties, with the goal of electing a left-liberal majority. The SPD leadership decided the party would support liberals in the second-round run-off elections, insisting on only one programmatic condition: that the candidates oppose indirect taxes. With one of these parties, the Progressives, the SPD went further, abandoning even their one condition in order to negotiate a deal for mutual support in the second-round voting. The deal saved the declining Progressives, who ended up owing 80 percent of their parliamentary seats to SPD support. Yet in districts allocated to the SPD in the agreement, few Progressive voters supported the socialist candidates. After the elections, the hope of a left-liberal bloc in the Reichstag quickly vanished, as the liberals aligned themselves with the right-wing parties.

13. In 1906, a rebellion occurred in the German colonies of South West Africa (now known as Namibia) and East Africa (now largely Tanzania) as tribes such as the Herreros and the Khoikhoi (called "Hottentots" by southern African whites) rose up against the cruelty of the colonial administration. The German troops sent to quell the uprising were ordered to indiscriminately massacre the natives. It is estimated that out of the total population of 80,000 Herreros, 60,000 were killed. Tens of thousands of other Africans were also killed. The SPD attacked the cruelty of government colonial policy and protested these massacres. In response, the landlord and capitalist parties temporarily put aside their own conflicts and organized a chauvinist crusade in the 1907 elections; the

SPD suffered a sharp electoral defeat. Right-wing SPD leaders concluded that the party should steer away from criticism of imperial foreign policy in the future. The left stressed that more energetic anti-imperialist education was needed.

14. Prince Bernhard von Bülow (1849–1929) was German chancellor from 1900 until 1909.

15. Franz Mehring (1846–1919) was a German Marxist who in addition to his political and journalistic tasks wrote widely on history and helped organize and publish the works of Marx and Engels. Mehring was a leader of the left wing of German social democracy and a founder of the Spartacus League and the German Communist Party.

16. In July 1911, while French troops were establishing a protectorate over Morocco in Northwest Africa, a German warship steamed into the Moroccan harbor of Agadir to land troops against the French. For a while war seemed imminent, with Britain siding with France. The crisis was settled in November when Germany recognized France's protectorate in Morocco, in return for territorial concessions from France in Equatorial Africa.

When the crisis first broke out, Camille Huysmans (1871–1968), a Belgian socialist and secretary of the Second International (who later became a rabid chauvinist and a minister in the Belgian government), sent a letter to all sections of the International. It asked whether they thought an emergency meeting should be held of the International Socialist Bureau, the executive committee of the Socialist International.

Hermann Molkenbuhr replied on behalf of the SPD, opposing the calling of such a meeting. Reflecting the opportunists' conclusions from the 1907 election, he explained: "If we should prematurely engage ourselves so strongly [as to go on record through an International meeting] and even give precedence to the Morocco question over questions of internal [domestic] policy, so that an effective electoral slogan could be developed against us, then the consequences will be unforeseeable."

This letter was made public by Rosa Luxemburg, who published it in the *Leipziger Volkszeitung*, along with a vigorous denunciation of it and the policy it represented.

17. Sidney (1859–1947) and Beatrice (1858–1943) Webb authored numerous books and were leading figures in the bourgeois-liberal Fabian Society in Britain. Sidney Webb later became colonial minister in the British government formed by the Labour Party, 1929–31.

18. The German trade unions were designated as "free" to distinguish them from the "yellow" company unions and the Catholic unions.

19. Philip Scheidemann (1865–1937) and Friedrich Ebert (1870–1925) were the two central figures in the SPD who led the party into support of the German imperialist war effort, expelled the party's left wing, and presided over the crushing of the German revolution in 1918–19. They both entered Kaiser Wilhelm's cabinet in the last days of the war in an attempt to save the German monarchy. In the bourgeois republic established in 1919, Scheidemann became chancellor and Ebert became president.

Karl Legien (1861–1920) was the social democratic head of the German trade unions from 1890 until his death. Wilhelm Pfannkuch was a member of the SPD executive committee who held centrist political views.

20. Here Zinoviev is not referring to the big monopoly capitalists and their top managerial staff, but to all those—large or small—who hire labor and live off profits.

21. John Burns (1858–1943) was president of the Local Government Board in the British Liberal government from 1906 to 1914. Arthur Henderson (1863–1935) was secretary of the British Labour Party 1911–34 and president of the Second International in the twenties; he was instrumental in securing Labour support for British war policy in World War I. Andrew Fisher (1862–1928) served as Australian prime minister three times between 1908 and 1915 at the head of the Labor Party government.

22. The German mark was then worth approximately US$.25; by today's price index it would be worth about $2.50. By this standard, 10,000 marks in 1916 would be equivalent to about $25,000 today.

23. *Vorwärts* was the daily newspaper of the SPD under the control of the Berlin party organization. In 1916 this organization was a stronghold of the SPD's militant working-class opposition. Many revolutionary-minded workers were still aligned with centrist leaders like Kautsky; many more were turning to the left-wing Spartakusbund led by Liebknecht and Luxemburg. Under the control of the Berlin oppositionists, *Vorwärts* strongly opposed the government and was critical of the SPD majority leadership. In October 1916 the government suppressed *Vorwärts*. The military command would only let the paper reappear if there was a change in its editorship. The paper reopened after ten days under the control of the SPD majority leadership. It later turned out that this whole procedure had been suggested to the government by the SPD leadership.

Berlin workers were indignant over the theft of their newspaper, which was a major step toward the split of the SPD. In January 1917 the right wing expelled the oppositionists, most of whom united to form the Independent Social Democratic Party (USPD). But this grouping in turn was torn by the political conflict between those such as Liebknecht and Luxemburg who aimed to overcome the war crisis by establishing workers' rule, and those like Kautsky who wanted only to protest the chauvinist and proimperialist excesses of the majority. At the end of 1918, two months after the opening of the German revolution, the Spartacists joined with independent groups of revolutionary workers to form the Communist Party of Germany.

24. W.A. Holman and Joseph Cook (1860–1947) were leaders of the Australian Labor Party. Cook was prime minister in 1913–14.

25. Thorvald Stauning (1873–1942) was chairman of the

Danish Social Democratic Party and entered the government in 1916, serving as prime minister 1924–26 and 1929–40.

26. Wilhelm Liebknecht (1826–1900) had been a member of the early Communist League founded in 1847 with Marx and Engels's participation, and the First International, which Marx and Engels also played a key role in helping to establish in 1864. Liebknecht was a founder of German social democracy in 1869. He was a friend and collaborator of Marx and Engels and remained a central leader of the Social Democratic Party until his death. He was the father of Karl Liebknecht.

27. Anton Pannekoek (1873–1960) joined the Dutch Social Democratic Workers Party in 1902. As a leader of the left-wing faction, he was expelled in 1909 and helped found a small left-socialist party. During the war Pannekoek participated in the Zimmerwald Left led by Lenin, and was a co-founder of the Dutch Communist Party in 1918. A proponent of ultraleft views, he left the party in 1921.

28. Georg von Vollmar (1850–1922), a former army officer, became in 1890 the first open advocate of revisionism in the German Social Democratic Party. In 1898 he helped put together an electoral alliance with the Catholic Center Party in Bavaria, which was criticized by the SPD nationally.

29. Maximilien Robespierre (1758–1794) was one of the outstanding leaders of the French bourgeois revolution. As leader of the left Jacobins, he headed the revolutionary government in 1793–94. Robespierre was overthrown and guillotined by a counterrevolutionary coup on the ninth of Thermidor, July 27, 1794.

30. During the late 1880s, a wave of workers' struggles in Britain brought thousands of unskilled workers, previously unorganized, into the trade unions. The idea that the unions should organize these layers was dubbed the "new trade unionism"—as opposed to the "old trade unionism," where the trade unions were viewed as the exclusive domain of the skilled crafts.

31. William M. Hughes (1864–1952) was an Australian

union official and Labor Party leader who served as prime minister from 1915 to 1923.

32. V.M. Purishkevitch (1870–1920), a Russian big landowner and monarchist, founded the ultrareactionary and anti-Semitic Black Hundreds.

33. Heinrich Cunow (1862–1936), considered an "orthodox Marxist" before the war, became a social patriot and was the main "theoretician" of the Scheidemann group in the SPD's right-wing leadership. Paul Lensch (1873–1926) was an SPD left-winger who also became a chauvinist in 1914, eventually leaving the SPD and becoming an editor for a leading German industrialist. August Winning (1878–?) was a leading revisionist in the SPD.

34. Otto Bauer (1881–1938) was a central leader of the Austrian Social Democrats and the chief theoretician of what became known as "Austro-Marxism," whose positions on the national and colonial questions were sharply attacked by Lenin. He took a centrist position during the war, but became minister of foreign affairs in the coalition government established after the war following the overthrow of the Austrian monarchy.

35. Kurt Eisner (1887–1919) was a revisionist who opposed the war on pacifist grounds and became affiliated to the centrist USPD following the split. Installed by the 1918 revolution as prime minister of Bavaria, he was assassinated by an army officer.

36. Max Schippel (1859–1928) was a right-wing revisionist within the SPD. In the 1890s, he published a work revising Engels's view on militarism, alleging that the German working class had an interest in the growth of German militarism. As a member of the Reichstag, he openly defended the policy of German imperialism.

37. Friedrich Naumann (1860–1919) was a Protestant theologian and liberal member of the Reichstag. As a leading publicist, he propagandized for German imperialism.

38. Maximilian Harden (1861–1927), Ludwig Stelin, and

Werner Sombart (1863–1941) were prominent bourgeois opponents of Marxism.

39. Max Weber (1864–1920) was a German sociologist who, while claiming acceptance of certain aspects of Marxism, propounded an anti-Marxist doctrine that has been influential in modern sociology. Instead of the class struggle and the development of the productive forces of society, Weber gave primary weight to religious ideology and charismatic leaders as shapers of social development.

New International
A MAGAZINE OF MARXIST POLITICS AND THEORY

NEW INTERNATIONAL NO. 12
Capitalism's Long Hot Winter Has Begun
JACK BARNES

Today's global capitalist crisis is but the opening stage of decades of economic, financial, and social convulsions and class battles. Class-conscious workers confront this historic turning point for imperialism with confidence, Jack Barnes writes, drawing satisfaction from being "in their face" as we chart a revolutionary course to take power. $14. Also in Spanish, French, Farsi, Arabic, and Greek.

NEW INTERNATIONAL NO. 14
Setting the Record Straight on Fascism and World War II
STEVE CLARK

World War II was not "a popular war against Fascism." It was several wars in one. It was a massacre by imperialism in order to redivide the world. It was a war to defend the Soviet Union against attempts by the capitalist powers to undo the world's first socialist revolution. It gave impetus to struggles for national liberation throughout the world. The book sets apart myths from reality concerning the causes and the results of these wars, and shows how communists in the United States charted a revolutionary course of class struggle as they were unfolding. $14. Also in Spanish and French.

NEW INTERNATIONAL NO. 13
Our Politics Start with the World
JACK BARNES

The huge economic and cultural inequalities between imperialist and semicolonial countries, and among classes within them, are accentuated by the workings of capitalism. To build parties able to lead a successful revolutionary struggle for power in our own countries, vanguard workers must be guided by a strategy to close this gap. $14. Also in Spanish, French, Farsi, and Greek.

NEW INTERNATIONAL NO. 10
Imperialism's March toward Fascism and War
JACK BARNES

"There will be new Hitlers, new Mussolinis. That is inevitable. What is not inevitable is that they will triumph. The working-class vanguard will organize our class to fight back against the devastating toll we are made to pay for the capitalist crisis. The future of humanity will be decided in the contest between these contending class forces." $14. Also in Spanish, French, Farsi, and Greek.

NEW INTERNATIONAL NO. 11
U.S. Imperialism Has Lost the Cold War
JACK BARNES

The collapse of regimes across Eastern Europe and the USSR claiming to be communist did not mean workers and farmers there had been crushed. In today's sharpening capitalist conflicts and wars, these toilers are joining working people the world over in the class struggle against exploitation. $14. Also in Spanish, French, Farsi, and Greek.

NEW INTERNATIONAL NO. 7
Opening Guns of World War III: Washington's Assault on Iraq
JACK BARNES

Washington's murderous 1991 war on Iraq heralded conflicts among imperialist powers, growing capitalist crisis, and spreading wars. Working people in the region—from the Kurds, to Palestine and Israel, to Iran, Iraq, and Syria—are fighting for space to defend national rights and class interests. $14. Also in Spanish, French, and Farsi.

WWW.PATHFINDERPRESS.COM

UNIONS: THEIR PAST, PRESENT, AND FUTURE

Trade Unions in the Epoch of Imperialist Decay
LEON TROTSKY, FARRELL DOBBS, KARL MARX

"The trade unions can be really independent of the capitalist state only to the extent that they are conscious of being, in addition, the organs of proletarian revolution." $15

Labor's Giant Step
The First Twenty Years of the CIO: 1936–55
ART PREIS

The story of the explosive labor struggles and political battles in the 1930s that built the industrial unions. And how those unions became the vanguard of a mass social movement that began transforming US society. $27

The Great Labor Uprising of 1877
PHILIP S. FONER

In 1877 a battle by West Virginia rail workers against wage cuts effectively shut down the US rail system and turned into the country's first nationwide general strike. Welcomed by Karl Marx as the "first eruption against the oligarchy of associated capital" since the US Civil War, the uprising coincided with the bourgeoisie's betrayal of Radical Reconstruction in the South and the first steps in the rise of US imperialism and its counterrevolutionary course worldwide. $17

INDEX

A
Adams, Gerry, 38
Affirmative action, 17, 137
AFL-CIO, 8, 39–40. *See also* Labor bureaucracy
Africa: colonial revolution in, 26, 31, 152–53; imperialist interventions in, 56, 84, 237; nuclear weapons and, 58; South West Africa rebellion (1906), 236
Alarcón, Ricardo, 14
Algeria, 31
American Federation of Labor (AFL), 129, 144–45, 192
Anarchism, 108
Andropov, Yuri, 79–80
Anti-Dühring (Engels), 112–13
Anti-Semitism, 172
Anti–Vietnam War movement, 19, 20, 48–49, 87; comparisons with Central America and Caribbean, 21, 49; SWP and, 20, 48
Arab-Israeli war (1973), 57
Argentina, 159; and Malvinas war, 13, 14, 33–34, 35, 49, 84
"Arms race," 53, 72
Australia, 192–94, 209, 238

B
Banking, 103
Bauer, Otto, 217–22, 241
Bay of Pigs, 31
Bebel, August, 66, 171, 172, 173, 235; on labor aristocracy, 195; and opportunists, 180, 199
Belgium, 231
Berger, Victor, 129
Bernstein, Eduard, 126, 230
Bismarck, Otto von, 234
Blacks, 39, 58; in Britain, 51; capitalist oppression of, 20; and civil rights movement, 8, 133; racist prejudice against, 116, 129, 209; SWP and, 151–52
Blank, R., 235
Bolshevik Party, 81, 110, 121, 124, 139; and fight against imperialist war, 21–24, 45, 60, 101, 102, 232; and working class, 130, 140, 145, 147
Borchardt, Julian, 183
Bowley, E.L., 203–4
Brassey, Thomas, 207
Brazil, 34
Britain: antimissiles movement in, 46, 65, 67, 69; and anti–Vietnam War protests, 48; composition of working class in, 17, 51, 116–17; as imperialist power, 31, 34, 104; and Ireland, 14, 38–39, 116–17; labor aristocracy in, 105–6, 126, 202–8, 212, 213; and Malvinas war, 13, 14, 33–34,

247

35, 37–38, 40–41, 49, 50–51, 57, 84; as nuclear power, 28, 46, 52, 57, 70–71, 71–72; unions in, 39, 105, 106, 125–26, 191, 204, 240; and U.S. war in Central America, 14, 39, 50–51; working-class struggles in, 37–38, 105
Britt, Harry, 64
Bülow, Bernhard von, 174, 177, 237
Burns, John, 184, 206, 238
Bush, George, 41

C

Campaign for Nuclear Disarmament (CND), 51, 53, 65, 69
Canada, 133
Capital (Marx), 111–12, 114–15, 116, 208
Capitalism: antidemocratic character of, 7, 173; economic downturns in, 8, 136–37; monopoly, 103, 104, 149; no peaceful replacement of, 126; simple and complex labor under, 112–15; standing army under, 224; and working class, 8, 110, 111, 122, 134, 203–4. *See also* Imperialism
Castro, Fidel, 81–82, 83, 84, 87–88
Center Party (Germany), 169, 234
Central America and Caribbean, 39, 58, 152; and anti-intervention movement in U.S., 20–21, 39–40, 61, 64–65, 90; at center of world politics, 4, 15; escalating U.S. war in, 13–15, 21, 49, 50, 55, 84; world stakes in, 4, 83. *See also* Cuba; El Salvador; Grenada; Nicaragua
Central Intelligence Agency (CIA), 8

Chad, 56
Champion, Henry Hyde, 206, 207–8
Chiang Kai-shek, 36
Child labor, 116, 222, 223
Chile, 159
China, 35–36, 37, 57, 129; immigrants from, 129; revolution in, 24, 26, 29, 31, 74
Church, 78
Cold war, 7
Colonialism, 106, 132, 206–7; Second International debate on, 128–29. *See also* Imperialism
Colonial revolution, 17, 26, 29, 55, 74; sectarianism toward, 35–36
Communist International, 101, 102, 108, 124; on origins of opportunism, 106–7; Stalinist degeneration of, 25, 148; on trade unions, 142, 144, 145–46
Communist Manifesto (Marx and Engels), 124
Communist parties, 6, 146; orientation to most oppressed proletarian layers, 9, 17, 61, 140, 146, 148, 151–52; proletarianization of, 16–18, 61, 89; trade unionist vs. communist politics, 125, 147; and unions, 141–44, 150; working-class character of, 170–72, 213. *See also* Socialist Workers Party
Communist Party (Germany), 239
Communist Party, Great Britain, 60
Communist Party of Cuba, 83
Communist Party U.S.A., 144–45; class collaborationism of, 48–49, 59, 60, 68
Conditions of the Working Class in England, The (Engels), 203

Congo, 31
Conscription: under capitalism, 46; in Eastern Europe, 79, 82; in Nicaragua, 77
Conservative Party (Britain), 207–8
Conservative Party (Germany), 169, 234
Cook, Joseph, 192, 239
Croatia, 78–79
Cuba: labor aristocracy in, 159; on Malvinas, 35, 36; "missile crisis" in (1962), 55, 57; and proletarian internationalism, 79, 81; revolutionary victory in, 24, 26, 29; and Soviet Union, 55, 74; Territorial Troop Militia in, 77; U.S. attacks and threats, 14–15, 31; and world revolution, 5, 74, 78
Cunow, Heinrich, 213, 241
Czechoslovakia, 81

D

Daily Citizen, 191
Daily Mail, 191
David, Eduard, 168, 234
Debs, Eugene V., 129
Defeatism, revolutionary, 21–22, 101
Democratic Party: CP support for, 59, 60; "peace candidates" of, 48–49, 68; union officials' support for, 149
Democratic rights, 7, 64, 173
Democratic Socialists of America, 68
Denmark, 193–94, 239–40
Disarmament: and bourgeois peace movements, 47–48; of nuclear weapons, 44, 52, 53, 71–72; utopianism of, 44, 45–46, 51–52
Dominican Republic, 31

E

Eastern Europe, 70, 78–81; "independent peace movements" in, 76–77, 79; overturn of capitalism in, 24, 25, 26, 29, 74. *See also* Soviet Union
Ebert, Friedrich, 183, 238
Eckstein, Gustave, 201
Economism, 123–25, 141
Egypt, 57
Eisner, Kurt, 220, 241
Electoralism, bourgeois, 60, 193; of German Social Democrats, 176, 179–80, 237; and lesser-evil politics, 64–65, 66, 67–68, 69; referenda and ballot initiatives, 64–66, 67
Elm, Adolf von, 185
El Salvador, 14, 15. *See also* Central America and Caribbean
Engels, Frederick, 124, 203, 233–34; on administration by the people, 66–67; on housing question, 153–54; on labor aristocracy, 9, 104, 205, 206–8; on U.S. working class, 117–18
Equal Rights Amendment (ERA), 63–64

F

Fabian Society, 207–8, 238
Farabundo Martí National Liberation Front/Revolutionary Democratic Front (El Salvador), 83
Farmers, 62, 113, 118, 127, 175
Fascism, 25, 149
Federation of Salvadoran Trade Unions (FENASTRAS), 39
First International, 111
Fisher, Andrew, 184, 192, 193–94, 209, 210, 238
Fourth International, 47, 148; proletarianization of parties in, 16–17, 18

France: military interventions by, 31, 56, 237; monopoly capitalism in, 103, 105; as nuclear power, 28, 70–71; workers movement in, 108, 230–31

G

Garment workers, 115–16

Germany, 234; antisocialist laws in, 170, 171, 234; bourgeoisie in, 166, 167, 168, 172, 176, 210, 234; disintegration of liberalism in, 166–67, 172, 176; as imperialist power, 212–13, 214–15, 236–37; labor aristocracy in, 169, 202–3, 209–10, 211–15, 227–28; monopoly capitalism in, 103, 105; revolution of 1848 in, 166, 233–34; revolution of 1918 in, 23–24; unions in, 183–84, 187–91, 209–10, 227, 238; in World War II, 25–26, 73. *See also* Social Democratic Party (Germany)

Germany, East, 82

Germany, West, 41, 46, 52

Gompers, Samuel, 144, 145, 192, 209, 210

Grenada, 14, 15, 24, 26, 27, 78

Guatemala, 14

H

Hall, Gus, 59, 60, 88

Hansen, Joseph, 71

Harden, Maximilian, 231, 241–42

Heine, Wolfgang, 168, 234

Henderson, Arthur, 184, 210, 238

Herkner, Heinrich, 190–91, 211

Hiroshima and Nagasaki, 26, 42, 74

Holland, 46, 198–99; labor aristocracy in, 208–9, 230–31

Holman, W.A., 192, 193, 239

Honduras, 13, 14, 65

Hughes, William M., 209, 240–41

Huysmans, Camille, 193, 237

I

Immigrant workers, 17, 116, 118–19, 144, 209; debate in Second International on, 129–30

Imperialism, 219–20; interimperialist rivalries, 28; no fear of, 86; and semicolonial world, 33–36, 158; as stage of capitalism, 32, 103–4, 109; superprofits from, 105–6, 132–33, 134, 150, 203; working class and, 214–16, 219–22. *See also* U.S. imperialism; War, imperialist

Imperialism: The Highest Stage of Capitalism (Lenin), 102–3, 118–19

In Defense of Marxism (Trotsky), 74

Indonesia, 31

Iran, 36–37

Iran-Iraq war, 36–37

Ireland, 38–39; Britain and, 14, 117

Israel, 31, 57, 69; as nuclear power, 28, 57

Italy, 46, 108, 230

J

Japan, 26, 35–36, 42, 52, 105

Junkers, 167, 200, 210–11, 234

K

Kampuchea, 37

Kautsky, Karl, 192; as centrist, 197, 201, 235, 239; on labor aristocracy, 203–5; on petty-bourgeois camp-followers, 175

Kenya, 31

Keufer, Auguste, 230–31

Khomeini, Ruhollah, 37

Kirkland, Lane, 40

Korea, 24, 29, 56
Korean War, 26, 31, 57

L

Labor aristocracy: formation of, 115; in Australia, 192–94, 209; in Britain, 105–6, 108–9, 126, 202–8, 212, 213; in colonial and semicolonial countries, 156–57, 159; in Germany, 169, 195, 202–3, 209–10, 211–15; in Holland, 208–9, 230–31; and imperialist superprofits, 104, 105–6, 107, 134, 150, 157, 203, 205, 212–13, 221, 222–24; and job trusts, 8, 115, 152, 159, 182, 193; and labor bureaucracy, 9, 107, 131–32, 138–39, 146, 160, 184, 195, 223; Lenin on, 9, 104–6, 118–19, 130, 131–32, 140–41, 143, 148, 157; and opportunism, 5, 131–32, 140–41, 148, 199, 202–3, 206–7, 213–15, 230–31; real vs. transitory interests of, 134, 135, 139, 140, 146–47, 150, 216, 223–24; in U.S., 9, 118–19, 152, 209. See also Labor bureaucracy; Unions; Working class
Labor bureaucracy, 200–201; bourgeois intelligentsia in, 191; in Britain, 38, 40, 105, 106, 125–26, 181, 191; as caste, 107, 139, 181, 182, 193, 196–99, 201–2; class-collaborationist perspective, 5, 7–8, 9, 126, 143, 149, 150, 196–98, 200–201; in Germany, 183, 184, 185, 187–90, 201; labor aristocracy its base, 9, 107, 131–32, 138–39, 157, 160, 184, 223; as "labor lieutenants" of capitalism, 138, 158, 191–92, 210; recruited from labor aristocracy, 183–84, 192–93, 195,
224–25; salaries of, 183, 184; in semicolonial countries, 157–58; size and composition, 107, 183, 184, 185, 187–90; support to imperialism by, 8, 38, 40, 157; in U.S., 6–8, 191–92. See also Labor aristocracy; Unions
Labour Party (Britain), 33, 39, 152, 232, 238; and Ireland, 38; and Malvinas war, 40, 50–51; and nuclear disarmament, 46, 50, 52, 69
Landsberg, Otto, 168, 234
Laos, 24, 46
Lassalle, Ferdinand, 66
Latin America: imperialist interventions in, 31, 35, 84, 85–86; nuclear weapons and, 58. See also Central America and Caribbean; Malvinas war; individual countries
Lebanon, 4, 31
Left, petty-bourgeois, 151; and imperialist war drive, 48–49, 53, 54, 59, 64, 66, 72–73, 76
Legien, Karl, 183, 184, 210, 213, 214, 216, 238
Lenin, V.I., 81, 86, 90, 99, 121; on Economists, 123–25; on fight against imperialist war, 22, 23, 44, 60, 101, 232; on imperialism, 102–6; on labor aristocracy, 9, 104–6, 118–19, 130, 131–32, 140–41, 143, 148, 157; leads fight in Second International, 110, 126–30; on national wars, 30, 31–32, 33, 34; on Second International collapse, 102, 106–9, 139; on unions, 141–44; on working class in revolutionary struggle, 122–25, 147–48
Lensch, Paul, 213, 214, 215–16, 220, 241

Leon Trotsky on Black Nationalism and Self-Determination, 151
Liberalism, 166–67, 173, 207
Liberal Party (Britain), 69, 207, 208
Liberal People's Party (Germany), 169
Liebknecht, Karl, 235, 236, 239, 240
Liebknecht, Wilhelm, 66, 194, 195, 240
Livingstone, Ken, 38
Ludlow amendment, 62–63
Luxemburg, Rosa, 235–36, 238; polemic with Kautsky, 173, 201–2, 239

M

Malaya, 31
Malvinas war, 13, 14, 40–41, 49, 57, 84; support for Argentina in, 33–34, 35
Mann, Tom, 206
Manning, Cardinal, 206
Marx, Karl, 124, 233–34; on Ireland, 38, 116–17; on labor aristocracy, 9, 104, 115, 205–6, 207, 208; on simple and complex labor, 111–13, 114–15; on unions, 111, 120–21; on wages and profit, 135–36
Maslow, P.P., 220
Mehring, Franz, 174, 237
Mensheviks, 130
Mexico, 159
Michels, Robert, 195–96, 229
Militant Tendency (Britain), 33, 35
Military budget, 90, 178, 219; communist opposition to, 45–46
Mitterrand, François, 56
Molina Lara, Alejandro, 39–40
Molkenbuhr, Hermann, 179, 183, 237
Morocco, 179, 237

N

Namibia, 31, 236
National Liberal Party (Germany), 169, 234
Naumann, Friedrich, 231, 241
Neue Zeit, 201, 235
New Jewel Movement (Grenada), 83
Nicaragua: draft in, 77; labor aristocracy in, 159; on Malvinas, 35; revolution, 24, 26, 78, 81; U.S. war against, 13–15, 85–86
North Atlantic Treaty Organization (NATO), 52, 55, 70
Nuclear power, 43
Nuclear war, 86, 88; imperialism and, 4, 41–42, 47, 54; petty-bourgeois left on, 53, 54, 59
Nuclear weapons, 26–28, 41–44, 52–61, 57; Britain and, 28, 46, 52, 57, 70–71, 71–72; petty-bourgeois left on, 53, 54, 58–59, 60; protests against, 46–47, 48, 51–52, 65, 67–69, 70–71; Soviet Union and, 26–28, 44, 70, 88; unilateral disarmament demand, 43–44, 45, 52, 71–72; U.S. arsenal of, 27, 28, 29, 52, 54–55, 56, 68, 70, 84; U.S. threats to use, 57–58; U.S. use of, 26, 42, 74, 86; world opposition to, 18, 42–43, 46–47

O

Opportunism, 233; and labor aristocracy, 5, 131–32, 138, 140–41, 148, 199, 202–3, 206–7, 213–15, 230–31; in Second International, 106, 108, 126–28, 165, 179, 200, 202–9, 237; social roots of, 104, 127, 131–32, 165–232

Ortega, Daniel, 85–86, 90

P

Pacifism, 47–49, 60, 71, 72–73, 76, 77
Palestinians, 57
Pannekoek, Anton, 196–98, 240
Paris Commune (1871), 23
Patriotism, bourgeois: adaptation to, 46, 101, 178–79, 213–15; in Germany, 173–79, 236–37; during Malvinas war, 38, 40; and petty bourgeoisie, 174, 175, 176, 178
Peace: bourgeois demagogy around, 50, 72; class-collaborationist approach to, 58–60, 83, 90; revolutionary road to, 4–5, 19–20, 47, 54, 60, 61, 62, 81–82, 83, 87–88, 89, 90–91; Stalinist appeals for, 59–60, 79–80, 81–82. *See also* War, imperialist, fight against
Peronism, 159
Petty bourgeoisie, 113; attraction to proletariat, 166–67, 172–73, 176; and bourgeois patriotism, 174, 175, 176, 178; and opportunism in Second International, 108, 127, 131–32, 168, 225–26, 228–30, 231–32; vacillations of, 168
Pfannkuch, Wilhelm, 183, 238
Pol Pot, 37
Poland, 78
Police, 45
Portugal, 133
PRI (Institutional Revolutionary Party, Mexico), 159
Progressive Party (Germany), 236
Protectionism, 126, 217–19, 221
Proudhon, Pierre-Joseph, 153–54
Purishkevitch, V.M., 211, 241

R

Reagan, Ronald, 41, 50, 55–56, 64, 72, 83
Revolutions of 1848, 166, 233–34
Rexhauser, Ludwig, 230
Robespierre, Maximilien, 202, 240
Rüdorffer (Kurt Rietzler), 176, 177, 178
Russia, 23, 166
Russian revolution (1917), 23–24, 25
Russian Social Democratic Labor Party (RSDLP), 122, 130

S

Sandinista National Liberation Front (FSLN), 83, 85
Scheidemann, Philip, 183, 184, 186, 187, 210, 213, 238
Schippel, Max, 220, 221, 241
Schmoller, Gustav von, 210, 211, 213, 230
Schulze-Gaevernitz, Gerhard von, 212
Second International: betrayal by, 23, 100, 101, 102, 104, 106–7, 109, 139, 165, 232; centrists in, 108, 129, 139, 201–2, 217, 235; currents in, 107–8, 232–33; debate at congresses of, 23, 100, 127–30; growth of opportunism in, 106, 108, 126–28, 165, 179, 200, 202–9, 237; International Socialist Bureau of, 179, 237; and labor aristocracy, 5, 108, 148, 202–3; revolutionary wing in, 108, 110, 126, 130, 233. *See also* Social Democratic Party (Germany)
Semicolonial countries: class struggle in, 156–60; imperialist wars against, 33–36; national liberation struggles in, 29, 32

Sinn Fein, 38
Sino-Japanese War, 35–36
Social Democratic Party (Austria-Hungary), 232, 241
Social Democratic Party (Britain), 69
Social Democratic Party (Germany): betrayal in 1914 by, 100, 198, 201, 232; bureaucracy in, 183, 184–87, 189–90, 194, 195–99; camp-followers of, 131, 166–81, 199; electoral results of, 169–70, 173–74, 176, 180, 196, 236; electoralism of, 176, 179–80, 237; "Marxist center" in, 173, 235; membership of, 180, 196, 199; and Morocco crisis (1911), 179, 237; and 1907 "Hottentot elections," 173–77, 236–37; opportunism in, 128, 131–32, 166–72, 178–81, 187, 199, 200–201, 230, 237; petty-bourgeois members in, 225–26, 228–30, 231–32; Reichstag fraction, 168, 172, 180, 190; working-class membership, 170, 225, 226–27, 228; working-class opposition in, 239; youth organization of, 186–87
Social democrats, 133, 233; antiwar and antimissiles movements and, 48–49, 58–59, 60–61, 68
Socialistische Monatschefte, 211
Socialist Party (France), 232
Socialist Party (U.S.), 129–30
Socialist Workers Party (SWP, U.S.), 61–63; in anti-Vietnam War movement, 20, 48; on bilateral nuclear freeze, 68–69; and Black workers, 151–52; proletarianization of, 17–18; union fractions, 20, 90. *See also* Communist parties
Social Revolution, The (Kautsky), 203–4, 204–5

Sombart, Werner, 231, 241–42
South Africa, 57
Soviet Union: defense of workers state in, 70, 71, 73–75, 77, 78; degeneration of revolution in, 25; and fight for "peace," 59–60, 79–80, 81–82; as imperialist target, 24, 29, 55, 56, 81; myth of "expansionism" by, 25, 72, 73, 75–76; as nuclear power, 26–28, 44, 70, 88; as obstacle to imperialist war, 24–25, 27–28, 57; planned economy in, 27, 73, 75; Stalinist bureaucracy in, 59–60, 73, 81; workers in, 80–81; in World War II, 25–26, 73, 81
Spain, 108
Spartacus League (Germany), 239
Sports, 205
Stalin, Joseph, 81
Stauning, Thorvald, 193, 239–40
Stelin, Ludwig, 231, 241–42
Südekum, Albert, 168, 180, 210, 213, 234
Switzerland, 66–67, 230

T

Taxes, 176, 219, 236
Thatcher, Margaret, 33, 40–41, 49, 72, 75–76, 152
Thompson, E.P., 53, 54, 58–59, 69, 71
Three Mile Island, 43
Tönnies, Ferdinand, 190
"Trade Unions in the Epoch of Imperialist Decay" (Trotsky), 149–51, 156–60
Transitional Program, 44, 61, 148
Trotsky, Leon, 69–70; on defense of Soviet Union, 73, 74, 75, 77, 78; on pacifism and war question, 44, 45–46, 48, 53–54, 62–63, 66,

86; on proletarianization, 17–18, 148, 151, 152; on semicolonial countries, 34–36, 156–59; on unions, 149–51, 156–59

U

Ultraleftism, 35, 142–43, 240
Unemployed, 8, 46, 111, 136–37, 146
Unions: in Britain, 39, 105, 106, 125–26, 191, 204, 240; and capitalist state, 149, 150, 151; communists in, 141–44, 150; craft outlook in, 119, 125, 143, 147; and defense of most oppressed, 17, 121, 147; and fight against racist and chauvinist discrimination, 17, 115, 124, 145; in Germany, 183–84, 187–91, 209–10, 227, 230, 238; need for organizational apparatus, 200; reason for being, 15, 111, 119–20, 142; in semicolonial countries, 157, 158; transformation into revolutionary instruments, 15–16, 89, 147; and unorganized workers, 119–20, 121, 141, 145, 227, 240; in U.S., 118, 119, 145; and U.S. war in Central America, 39–40, 61, 90; in western Europe, 230–31. *See also* Labor bureaucracy
United Mine Workers (UMW), 144
United States: Bring Us Home Movement in (1945), 26; domination by banks, 103; immigrant workers in, 17, 118–19; labor aristocracy in, 9, 118–19, 209; need for revolution in, 4–5, 47; why no labor party in, 152; working class in, 8–9, 117–19, 133. *See also* U.S. imperialism
U.S. imperialism: AFL-CIO and,

8; attacks on Cuba, 14–15, 31; bipartisan foreign policy of, 8, 15; and Central America and Caribbean, 13–15, 21, 40, 41, 49, 50, 55, 83, 84, 85–86; as dominant world power, 7, 26, 86; nuclear weapons of, 26, 27, 28, 29, 52, 56, 57–58, 68, 70, 84, 86; tactical divisions within, 15; and Vietnam War, 4, 19, 49–50, 83–84; war machine of, 46, 56, 72
USPD (Independent Social Democratic Party, Germany), 239

V

Vietnam, 29, 37. *See also* Anti-Vietnam War movement
"Vietnam syndrome," 28
Vietnam War: and antiwar movement, 49; revolutionary victory in, 4, 14, 17, 26, 31, 50, 74, 84, 87, 152; U.S. efforts in, 48, 49–50, 57; and war against French colonialism, 26, 31
Vollmar, Georg von, 199, 210, 240
Vorwärts, 186, 239

W

Wage Labour and Capital (Marx), 135–36
Wages, determination of, 112–13, 136–37
Wages, Price and Profit (Marx), 121
Walker, Nancy, 64
Waltershausen, Sartorius von, 211–13, 217
War, imperialist, 4, 49–50; against colonial peoples, 29–32; and communist strategic course, 16, 19–20, 22, 23, 43, 72, 102, 108; fight against, 15–16, 18–24, 69, 90; interimperialist, 28. *See also* Malvinas war; Peace; Viet-

nam War; World War I; World War II
War and the Fourth International (Trotsky), 78
Wars, national, 29, 30–33
Webb, Beatrice and Sidney, 181, 191, 238
Weber, Max, 231, 242
Weinberger, Caspar, 56
What Is To Be Done? (Lenin), 123–25, 141
Winning, August, 213, 214, 241
Women, 9, 20, 116, 204
Working class, 6–7, 20, 80–81, 108, 133, 152; capitalist exploitation of, 8, 110, 122, 134, 203–4; chauvinist influences on, 30, 32, 128–29, 144, 176–77; class interests of, 16, 21–22, 38, 72, 134, 135–36, 138–39, 140, 213–14; competition within under capitalism, 110–11, 137, 138; consciousness, 9, 20, 21, 22, 43, 49, 69, 72, 123–25, 152, 153, 159; divisions within, 114–17, 137, 138; and fight against imperialism, 15–16, 21, 29–30, 32, 88–89; imperialism and, 214–16, 219–22; independent political action of, 20, 65, 68, 89, 123, 133, 145; international solidarity of, 79, 117, 130, 137, 140, 215–16; most oppressed layers of, 9, 17, 115–16, 118, 119, 121, 140, 146, 151–52; rate of unionization in, 119–20; revolutionary capacity of, 133; in semicolonial countries, 157, 158; and skilled and unskilled labor, 111–13, 114–15; unskilled layers, 115, 119, 203, 204, 209, 225, 226–27, 228, 240; as vanguard of all oppressed, 17, 122–24, 147–48. *See also* Labor aristocracy; Labor bureaucracy; Unions
World War I, 21–24, 25, 47, 100
World War II, 7, 149; pacifists and, 47–48; Soviet Union in, 25, 26, 73, 81; U.S. victory in, 26

Y

Young workers, 9, 89, 145, 148, 223
Youth organization, socialist, 186–87
Yugoslavia, 78–79; revolution in, 24, 74

Z

Zimbabwe, 31
Zinoviev, Gregory, 5, 99, 131–32, 165–232

The Militant

Socialist newsweekly
published in the
interests of
working people

- Covers labor battles and workers fights for jobs, safety, and to organize the unorganized around the world.

- Reports on fights against cop brutality and frame-ups, against attacks on women's right to choose abortion, and for amnesty for workers who are foreign born.

- Explains the roots of the worldwide crisis of the capitalist system, and the never-ending imperialist interventions and wars as the old order unravels.

- Defends the socialist revolution in Cuba. Champions the fight to end Washington's economic embargo against Cuba and to demand US out of Guantánamo. Supports the fight against US colonial rule in Puerto Rico.

- Reports weekly campaigning by Socialist Workers Party members on workers' doorsteps and the road forward they explain for the working class to take political power out of the hands of the capitalist rulers.

The Militant • 306 West 37th Street, 13th floor • New York, NY 10018

Subscribe today!
New readers 12 weeks for $5
6 months $20   1 year $35   2 years $65

WWW.THEMILITANT.COM

EXPAND YOUR REVOLUTIONARY LIBRARY

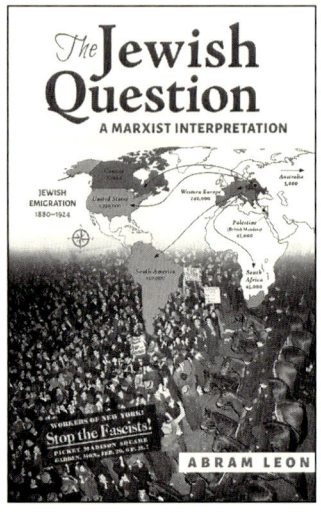

The Jewish Question
A Marxist Interpretation
ABRAM LEON

Why is Jew-hatred still raising its ugly head? What are its class roots—from antiquity through feudalism, to capitalism's rise and current crises? Why is there no solution under capitalism? The author, Abram Leon, was killed in the Nazi gas chambers. Revised translation, new introduction, and 40 pages of illustrations and maps. $17. Also in Spanish and French.

Che Guevara Talks to Young People

Guevara challenges the youth of Cuba and the world to work. To become disciplined. To join the vanguard on the front lines of struggles, small and large. To become a different kind of human being as they fight together with working people of all lands to transform the world. $12. Also in Spanish and Greek.

The Rise and Fall of the Nicaraguan Revolution

Based on ten years of socialist journalism from inside Nicaragua, this special issue of *New International* recounts the achievements and worldwide impact of the 1979 Nicaraguan revolution. It traces the political retreat of the Sandinista National Liberation Front leadership that led to the downfall of the workers and farmers government in the closing years of the 1980s. Documents of the Socialist Workers Party by Jack Barnes, Steve Clark, and Larry Seigle. In *New International* no. 9. $14. Also in Spanish.

Puerto Rico: Independence Is a Necessity
RAFAEL CANCEL MIRANDA

One of the five Puerto Rican Nationalists imprisoned by Washington for more than 25 years and released in 1979 speaks out on the brutal reality of US colonial domination, the example of Cuba's socialist revolution, and the ongoing struggle for independence. $5. Also in Spanish and Farsi.

Capitalism's World Disorder
Working-Class Politics at the Millennium
JACK BARNES

The social devastation and financial crises, the coarsening of politics, the cop brutality and acts of imperialist aggression accelerating around us—all are products not of something gone wrong with capitalism but of its lawful workings. Yet the future can be changed by the united struggle and selfless action of working people conscious of their power to transform the world. $20. Also in Spanish and French.

Maurice Bishop Speaks
The Grenada Revolution and Its Overthrow, 1979–83

The triumph of the 1979 revolution in the Caribbean island of Grenada under the leadership of Maurice Bishop gave hope to millions throughout the Americas. Invaluable lessons from the workers and farmers government destroyed by a Stalinist-led counterrevolution in 1983. $20

WWW.PATHFINDERPRESS.COM

February 1965: The Final Speeches

MALCOLM X

Our revolt is not "simply a racial conflict of Black against white, or a purely American problem. Rather, we are seeing a global rebellion of the oppressed against the oppressor, the exploited against the exploiter." Speeches and interviews from the last three weeks of Malcolm X's life. $17

50 Years of Covert Operations in the US

Washington's Political Police and the American Working Class

LARRY SEIGLE, FARRELL DOBBS, STEVE CLARK

How class-conscious workers have fought against the drive to build the "national security" state essential to maintaining capitalist rule. $10. Also in Spanish and Farsi.

Genocide against the Indians

GEORGE NOVACK

Why did the leaders of the Europeans who settled in North America try to exterminate the peoples already living there? How was the campaign of genocide against the Indians linked to the expansion of capitalism in the United States? Noted Marxist George Novack answers these questions. $5. Also in Farsi.

Labor, Nature, and the Evolution of Humanity
The Long View of History

FREDERICK ENGELS, KARL MARX, GEORGE NOVACK, MARY-ALICE WATERS

Why is it important to know that social labor, transforming nature, has been the motor force of humanity's evolution for millions of years? Because without that knowledge, working people are unable to see beyond the capitalist epoch, beyond the class exploitation that warps all human relations, ideas, and values. The dictatorship of capital had a beginning … and it will have an end. But only the revolutionary conquest of state power by the working class can open the door to a world free of capitalism's dog-eat-dog social reality. A world built on human solidarity. A socialist world. $12. Also in Spanish and French.

Feminism and the Marxist Movement

MARY-ALICE WATERS

Since the founding of the modern revolutionary workers movement nearly 150 years ago, Marxists have championed the struggle for women's rights and explained the economic roots in class society of women's oppression. "The struggle for women's liberation," Waters writes, "was lifted out of the realm of the personal, the 'impossible dream,' and unbreakably linked to the progressive forces of our epoch"— the working-class struggle for power. $5. Also in Farsi.

Thomas Sankara Speaks
The Burkina Faso Revolution, 1983–87

Under Sankara's guidance, Burkina Faso's revolutionary government led peasants, workers, women, and youth to expand literacy; to sink wells, plant trees, erect housing; to combat women's oppression; to carry out land reform; to join others worldwide to free themselves from the imperialist yoke. $20. Also in French.

WWW.PATHFINDERPRESS.COM

CUBA'S SOCIALIST REVOLUTION AND THE WORLD

Our History Is Still Being Written
The Story of Three Chinese Cuban Generals in the Cuban Revolution

ARMANDO CHOY, GUSTAVO CHUI, MOISÉS SÍO WONG, MARY-ALICE WATERS

"What was the key measure to uproot discrimination against Chinese and blacks in Cuba? It was the socialist revolution itself." New edition sheds light on Chinese Cubans' involvement in Cuba's internationalist course, including in Africa and Latin America. $15. Also in Spanish, French, Farsi, Greek, and Chinese.

Cuba and Angola: The War for Freedom
HARRY VILLEGAS ("POMBO")

The story of Cuba's unparalleled contribution to the fight to free Africa from the scourge of apartheid. And how, in the doing, Cuba's socialist revolution was strengthened. $10. Also in Spanish, Farsi, and Greek.

How Far We Slaves Have Come!
South Africa and Cuba in Today's World
NELSON MANDELA, FIDEL CASTRO

Speaking together in Cuba in 1991, Mandela and Castro discuss the role of Cuba in the history of Africa and Angola's victory over the invading US-backed South African army. That victory accelerated the fight to bring down the racist apartheid system. $7. Also in Spanish and Farsi.